AMERICANISM

THE FOURTH GREAT

WESTERN RELIGION

AMERICANISM
THE FOURTH GREAT
WESTERN RELIGION

David Gelernter

Doubleday

NEW YORK   LONDON   TORONTO   SYDNEY   AUCKLAND

PUBLISHED BY DOUBLEDAY

Copyright © 2007 by David Hillel Gelernter

All Rights Reserved

Published in the United States by Doubleday, an imprint of The Doubleday
Broadway Publishing Group, a division of Random House, Inc., New York.

DOUBLEDAY and the portrayal of an anchor with a dolphin are registered
trademarks of Random House, Inc.

ISBN 978-0-385-51312-8

PRINTED IN THE UNITED STATES OF AMERICA

For my Jane

CONTENTS

ACKNOWLEDGMENTS

My editor Adam Bellow has guided this manuscript wisely and patiently every step of the way, and I'm grateful. I tried out several of the ideas in this book during my stint as a columnist for the *Los Angeles Times*, and I thank Susan Brenneman and Nick Goldberg for helping me to refine them (but they don't necessarily endorse them!). I tried out even more of these ideas in the indispensable pages of the *Weekly Standard*; my thanks to Bill Kristol and the whole *Standard* staff, but especially to Claudia Anderson and Richard Starr. Ideas launched under the auspices of the Shalem Institute, Jerusalem (where I've served as a senior fellow in Jewish thought), have been essential to this project. My new colleagues at the American Enterprise Institute, where I'm a national fellow, are exceptionally generous with ideas and time; Michael Novak and Leon Kass (among other AEI fellows) are national treasures of the first order, and their work and conversation has helped me understand America, religion, and the Bible; I'm grateful also to Chris DeMuth, the AEI's director, for good guidance and generous support. I'm aware also, every day, of the generosity of Yale University, where I'm a professor of computer science. Yale promotes the development of public intellectuals and stands for freedom of thought and research in the proudest American tradition—and for liberal education in the best sense.

My deepest thanks are due to Neal Kozodoy—my teacher, my colleague, and my true friend. I tried out many of the main ideas of this book in *Commentary*-sponsored lectures and in *Commentary* essays, all of which Neal edited with his customary thoroughness, deep care, and deep thought. Of course all remaining errors are mine, but any good points are due largely to the people I've named, to Neal above all. And my thanks to Roger Hertog too, who has repeatedly taken it upon himself, out of pure generosity, to give me guidance and help. Neal and Roger together add up to one of the rarest phenomena in the universe, a purely unselfish force for good.

Lastly, my thanks to my two boys, Joshua and Daniel, for becoming young men who can be funny and smart about any topic whatever, who get every joke and understand the deep spiritual things that are hardest to convey; and to my parents for everything; and to my wife for even more.

David Gelernter
Yale University and American Enterprise Institute

"I BELIEVE IN AMERICA"

"I believe in America." Many people have said so over the generations. They are not speaking of a nation. They are expressing belief in an idea, and not just any idea but a religious idea of enormous, transporting power.

In this book I will argue that America is no secular republic; it's a biblical republic. Americanism is no civic religion; it's a biblical religion. Americanism doesn't merely announce the nation's ideals on its own authority; it speaks on behalf of the Bible and the Bible's God, as Lincoln did in his Second Inaugural Address. Its goal is for America to move forward "with firmness in the right, as God gives us to see the right," as Lincoln said in that same speech. That America is a biblical republic and Americanism a biblical religion—both facts are perfectly consistent with absolute religious freedom; both are supported by mountains of evidence. So how come nobody knows them? Is the evidence secret? Hardly. But we live in a secular age. No book will change that fact, but our secular prej-

udice can't change history either. If we look the facts in the face
and don't flinch, we will see *America the biblical republic* and
Americanism the biblical religion emerge clearly.

"America" is one of the most beautiful religious concepts
mankind has ever known. It is sublimely humane, built on
strong confidence in humanity's ability to make life better.
"America" is an idea that results from focusing the Bible and
Judeo-Christian faith like a spotlight's beam on the problem of
this life (not the next) in the modern world, in a modern nation. The ideas that emerge in a blaze of light center on liberty,
equality, and democracy for all mankind.

These ideas are often attributed to ancient Greece and to
eighteenth-century philosophy. I will show how they grew in
fact from the Bible, Judaism, and Christianity. They were present implicitly (unopened buds) in the Puritan America of the
early 1600s. During the revolutionary era the climate was right
for the buds to bloom. And they were beautiful. But they
reached maturity only decades later, under the ministration of
the greatest religious figure of modern centuries—who was
also President of the United States.

The religious idea called "America" *is* religious insofar as it
tells an absolute truth about the meaning of human life, a truth
that we must take on faith. ("We hold these truths to be self-
evident," says the Declaration of Independence. No proofs are
supplied.) I will try to show that the "American Religion," which
gives "America" its spiritual meaning, consists of an American
Creed in the context of a doctrine I will call American Zionism.
Virtually everyone agrees on the existence if not the details of
the Creed, but the phenomenon I call American Zionism has
been discussed by relatively few historians. I will try to show that

the American Religion incorporates the biblical ideas of a chosen people in a promised land. Those concepts are the source of America's (sometime) sense of divine mission; of her (not invariable yet often powerful) feeling of obligation to all mankind; of her democratic chivalry—her nagging awareness of a duty to help the weak against the strong. This "chivalry" has nothing to do with knights and ladies; it is a deep sense of duty to the suffering, and comes straight from American Zionism.

I will try to show how the American Religion was shaped by American history and how it shaped that history in turn—America's history and its religion in a centuries-long embrace.

And I will try to show that the American Religion is a global religion. Believers in America have lived all over the world. Some have believed with tormented desperation. Others have believed serenely, because the idea called "America" seemed profoundly humane and beautiful. Most did not believe in America as if it were God, but *did* believe as if America had chosen a divine mission and had the means to carry it out. For others the belief was more abstract: America only symbolized the facts that liberty, equality, and democracy could indeed become real on this earth and that human beings could *make* them real. And given the many who have believed, as well as the depth and fervor of their belief and the sublimity of the American idea (which I have yet to define precisely), this American Religion is a great religion.

No religion had ever before laid out these three political ideals as its creed: *Liberty. Equality. Democracy.* The great achievement of Americanism is to proclaim these three principles *and* their biblical origins, to proclaim them in America's own new scriptures—especially Lincoln's presidential speeches—and to make them real in a functioning nation. But Americanism goes further, to declare that these three principles are not the exclusive property of Americans or Christians or believers in God or descendants of white Europeans. According to the American Religion, they belong to all mankind, and Americans have a duty not merely to preach but to *bring* them to all mankind.

We are used to hearing the principles of this Creed described as philosophical and not religious. But no truth can be "philosophical" unless you are willing to be argued out of it. Not many Americans are willing to be argued out of their dearest national possessions. The intensity of belief in this Creed among people who have never heard a philosophical argument in their lives belies the assertion that these ideas are "philosophical." Those who think that Lincoln at Gettysburg was offering a *philosophical* address when he spoke of a nation "conceived in liberty" and of "the proposition that all men are created equal" and of a "government of the people, by the people, for the people" are deluded. In that speech Lincoln built, out of words, a sacred shrine for America's three fundamental ideals. It is one of the most beautiful shrines mankind has ever seen, and one of the holiest.

The American Religion is a biblical faith. In effect, it is an extension or expression of Judaism or Christianity. It is also separate from those faiths; you don't have to believe in the Bible or Judaism or Christianity to believe in America or the American Religion. Atheists and agnostics have been ardent believers. A few have believed in America the way Jews or Christians believe in God. Muslims and Hindus, Marxists and pagans have all been devout believers in Americanism.

Of course you can hum a melody from a Bach oratorio without converting to Christianity. But there is no denying that

Christianity inspired the melody, through the medium of Bach's genius. And there is no denying that Christianity inspired Americanism far more directly, through the medium of many thinkers, patriots, and geniuses.

★ ★ ★

My topic is Americanism and not Christianity; Americanism and not America. America, the vast democratic nation north of Mexico, south of Canada, is different from Americanism—a religion proclaiming liberty, equality, and democracy. But to understand Americanism, we need to know something about America too.

Today many thinkers assert that America is a secular republic; that secularism is, in fact, one of the great ideas on which this nation is built. I will try to show that America is, on the contrary, a *biblical* republic.

The Bible has no official status in America and never will. You can be a loyal American and never read the Bible, or you can read it and reject it. Yet repeatedly and in many eras we find Americans with the Bible on their minds, like a melody that keeps running through their heads that they can't shake. That's what I mean by "biblical republic": not a theocracy; not a nation ruled by biblical laws. My only definition is informal. *A biblical republic has the Bible on its mind.* A biblical republic is full of citizens who agree with Samuel Taylor Coleridge that "in the Bible, there is more that *finds* me than I have experienced in all other books put together."

Philosophers sometimes debate the role of reason versus revelation in the spread of political ideas. Whatever the source of the ideas we believe in, most people have no interest in philosophical arguments, whether or not they have ever heard one.

Most of us accept an idea as true if it *seems* true, if we "recognize" its truth in roughly the same way we recognize a familiar face. Resonance is the physical phenomenon that makes a C string hum when the same pitch sounds nearby. When we hear an assertion that makes something within *us* hum, the "resonance," that inner humming, tells us the idea is right. This internal resonance depends on how our minds are loaded: on what we experienced and were taught as small children; on our genes; and, according to the religious-minded, on our souls.

Those who accept Americanism do so mainly because we recognize its principles as true—not because anyone has ever *convinced* us they were true.

When people have the Bible on their minds, they are apt to "recognize" (to accept as true) assertions that remind them somehow of biblical verses, stories, ideas. It makes no difference whether the principles of Americanism came from the Bible or from philosophy—although there is plenty of reason to believe, as I'll discuss, that the Bible was the most important source by far. But since Americans have traditionally had the Bible on their minds, they have tended to accept the principles of Americanism on biblical and not on philosophical grounds—wherever they came from originally.

★   ★   ★

Americanism is often introduced as a religion—only to be demoted immediately to the status of a "civil religion" to be trotted out on public occasions, or a mere expression of patriotism. The American Religion is neither a mere civil religion nor a form of patriotism. We can tell by reflecting on the millions of people over the last hundred years who have said "I believe in America" with religious ardor although they were not Americans and lived far away. They were not expressing belief in some foreign country's public ceremonial or patriotic display.

Russian Jews in 1910, desperate to escape vicious state-sponsored Jew-hatred. Cheering French throngs in 1919, waiting to see President Woodrow Wilson go by, having just been released from an endless-seeming, grinding, murderous war, courtesy of American troops. Nazi victims in a dozen countries. Starving Europeans in the late 1940s. Berlin residents blockaded by the Soviets, dependent on a round-the-clock American airlift. Russian refuseniks rotting in prison. Polish labor leaders challenging the Soviet Union in the 1980s. Kurds fighting Saddam Hussein in the 1990s. Millions of Iraqis—Kurds, Shia, and Sunnis—this very day. "I believe in America" was a statement of religious faith among all these peoples, and others too. Of course American loyalists in South Vietnam also said "I believe in America." Chinese students demonstrating against Communist tyranny in Tienanmen Square said "I believe in America." Hungarians rebelling against communism did too, in 1956. *Their* beliefs were tragically misplaced. America let them down, cruelly. Yet for most of those who believed, America came through. Believing in America, these downtrodden, battered human beings were pledging allegiance to a theological idea of great depth and beauty and power.

If belief in America has inspired countless non-Americans, it has inspired innumerable Americans too—or settlers in lands that would one day be part of America. It has inspired them differently but just as deeply. Belief in America has inspired all sorts of remarkable feats over the roughly four centuries of American and proto-American existence.

You would need *some* sort of fierce determination to set off in a puny broad-beamed, high-pooped, painfully slow, nearly undefended seventeenth-century ship to cross the uncharted ocean to an unknown, unmapped world.

You'd need remarkable determination to push westward into the heartland farther and farther from settlement and safety.

You'd need ferocious bravado to provoke the dominant great power of the day on the basis of fairly flimsy excuses and ultimately declare war and proclaim your independence.

You'd need powerful, practically incandescent determination to keep fighting the Civil War after the South had won major battles and slaughtered vast numbers of Union soldiers and gained the sympathy of both leading western European powers. The Civil War cost more and more money, energy, and blood—and the Union just kept on fighting.

You'd need enormous determination to turn your back on the isolationism and antimilitarism that comes naturally to Americans and butt into World War I—and eventually to reject isolationism for the indefinite future, for the long twilight struggle, when you accepted the challenge of the Cold War against the Soviet Union.

The freedom and independence of Greece and Turkey occasioned America's entry into the Cold War. Neither one is a pressing American interest, *not exactly*. And what on earth made that Idaho or Nebraska farmer—the one whom British prime minister Tony Blair spoke about so feelingly in an eloquent address to Congress—believe that *he* was responsible for protecting the Iraqi people and the world from Saddam Hussein? What did it all have to do with *him*? *Americanism* connected that farmer to Saddam Hussein and Iraq: the hatred of America it occasions, the American chivalry it inspires.

Americanism is potent stuff. But exactly what is it?

★ ★ ★

Explaining the American Religion—how it developed, what it asserts and why—is my first goal in this book. Most thinkers say that Puritanism disappeared hundreds of years ago. I believe they are wrong. Puritanism *turned into* the American Religion, and it survives today in this altered form. Our quest to know the American faith must begin with Puritanism.

I will show how Americanism carried forward Puritan ideas about the new Israel, Puritan fascination with the Bible, Puritan intensity—and added new ideas that emerged from the old ones.

My second goal is to show how the Bible and Puritanism molded America as a potter molds wet clay. Some secularists don't like to face this fact. Others face it eagerly and respond with hatred; they call America the Puritan nation, the nation of religious fanatics.

They are right, and we should acknowledge the fact: America *was indeed* founded by religious fanatics. The Puritans who dominated those first English settlements, who did so much to shape this nation and its faith, were fiercely, fanatically dedicated to their God. They burned with the desire to live right and be near Him. Religious fanatics have a bad name nowadays. Muslim fanatics murder men, women, and children at random, with jagged shrapnel packed into bombs designed to cause the greatest possible pain and misery. And they claim to be doing God's work—a slander on every religious believer who ever lived.

But the Puritans who settled the New World were fanatics of a different order. They came to America because they chose *not* to fight it out in England; they did *not* want to foment rebellion or cause bloodshed. They were convinced that the English

monarchy was corrupt—and that their duty was to save it, not
destroy it. They would save it by setting up a model society that
England and the whole world could copy. These were men and
women with ordinary human affections who did not believe
that those affections should be suppressed for God's sake. Just
the opposite: God, they believed, was all for them.

The Pilgrims who landed at Plymouth, Massachusetts, in
1620 were "separatists," Puritans of the most fanatic type.
They were so fanatic, so intolerant, that in 1621 they held a
feast and invited the local pagans to share it with them. There
was a great thanksgiving celebration, wrote the Pilgrim Edward Winslow, "many of the Indians coming amongst us, and
amongst the rest their greatest king, Massasoyt with some
ninety men, whom for three days we entertained and feasted."

John Winthrop was a prominent early settler, another religious fanatic whose soul was a furnace fired with (*roaring* with)
faith in God. Aboard ship bound for New England, Winthrop
wrote a famous prediction about the settlement he was about to
found: "Wee must Consider that wee shall be as a Citty upon a
Hill, the eies of all people are upon us."

When his group arrived in the New World, Winthrop and his
fellow Puritans had a rough few months, as nearly all early settlers did. But he found time to write his wife that "I like so well
to be heer, as I doe not repent my comminge . . . I never fared
better in my life, never slept better, never had more content of
minde." These fanatics knew something that today's murderers
don't: they had the Bible on their minds, and the Bible says,
"Choose life and live!—you and your children" (Deut. 30:19).
Winthrop quoted just this verse in his famous shipboard fore-
cast. He was happy in the New World, except for one thing: his
wife and several of his children were still in England and

would join him later. "I want nothinge," he wrote to his wife, "but thee and the rest of my family."

These are the fanatics who founded this nation and sketched out the first rough drafts of the American Religion. They are fanatics we ought to know better. We won't understand America or Americanism until we do.

★   ★   ★

I will try to explain Americanism and introduce some of the people who conceived it. But this is neither a history book nor a group portrait. It is an essay in "folk philosophy"; it uses the past to illuminate the present. It has messages for three types of person.

For modern secularists: the American Religion is humanist in the best sense of the word. Its biblical roots are clear. Yet Americanism is also a religion that atheists (and those who are merely indifferent to traditional religion) can and do profess, ardently.

Christians and Jews ought not to see Americanism as a blasphemous replacement for Christianity or Judaism. Anyone can ask a theologian, "What does Christianity say about this problem?" If the answer is satisfying, it is incorporated into the questioner's religion. The American Religion is traditional religion's response to modern political reality. It is an extension to the structure of Judaism or Christianity, an extra room out back.

For Christians specifically: you built America and Americanism. In so doing you gave mankind one of the greatest gifts it has ever received. *Do not allow yourselves to be spiritually dispossessed in your own homes!* This country will never have an established, official religion; it will never abandon religious freedom. But neither should it be allowed to abandon its history and origins, or lie about them. Christians are (rightly) prohibited to preach Christianity in the public schools; *secularists should be prohibited to preach secularism too!*

For all Christians facing the dauntingly powerful secularist culture of the modern United States: be strong and of good courage.

This same message holds for people of any faith (or none) who object to the fanatical careerism—the enemy of spirituality—that has gripped this country by the throat. America must remember the intensity of its onetime love affair with spiritual things. Once that love lit the American landscape like a pillar of fire on a moonless night—or like moonlight on a gentle summer evening. The self-described "revolutionaries" of the late 1960s had many stupid ideas, but at least they were idealists. When their big plan for America as a socialist commune fell apart, most of them turned cynical—and here we are. But one day we will shake the whole tragic episode out of our hair, many books by many authors from now, and remember who we are.

And for American Jews, my own community: in some ways, Jews are the ultimate outsiders. Jews have lived in America since 1654, albeit in numbers too small to make much difference until the twentieth century. But in another sense that I will explain, Jews are America's ultimate insiders. It's no accident that a seventeenth-century Puritan leader should have written, regarding his fellow Puritans: "We are the children of *Abraham*; and therefore we are under *Abraham's* covenant."

★   ★   ★

The American Religion is a broad, deep, important topic, yet the literature is scanty. That tells us something interesting in itself. Americans used to know all about Americanism; they didn't need books like this one. They used to learn Americanism in school, discuss it with their parents or children, read it in the newspapers, hear it in their music, see it on the stage or screen, sing it, play it, inhale it. No longer. "First in war, first in peace, first in the hearts of his countrymen"—for centuries a grateful nation used this phrase to refer to George Washington. Not long ago I spoke to a nineteen-year-old sophomore at a top college, a thoughtful, articulate music student—who had never heard this phrase and had no idea to whom it referred. Many of this nation's public school teachers object to Americanism on principle—although they have no idea what it is.

In 1913 the English poet Rupert Brooke traveled from England to New York and met a "charming American youth" aboard ship. "In America one man's just as good as another," said the charming youth to Brooke. "You'll never understand America . . . Would you like to hear me recite to you the Declaration of Independence?" Yes, said Brooke. The recitation commenced.

Many "charming youths" are proud of their countries, or used to be. But not many are (or ever were) able to recite the principles upon which their nations are based—for obvious reasons. Most nations are based on no principles; they are based instead on shared descent or ethnicity. The United States is different. It has a religion because it must have. Without one, it is a band of displaced persons and little more. In his inauguration as president, George Washington added the Bible to the ceremony—took the oath on the Bible although the Constitution doesn't say to do so. It was an intuitive *unifying* gesture, binding together Presbyterians and Episcopalians, Congregationalists and Lutherans, Quakers and Baptists and Catholics, and even deists like Jefferson, who admired and quoted the Bible. (In his own Second Inaugural Lincoln advanced this idea of spiritual unification to the highest plane.)

A religion must be taught to each new generation or it disappears. American culture used to teach implicitly what "I believe in America" means. American schoolchildren used to learn the Declaration of Independence and the Gettysburg Address. They used to sing, "Mine eyes have seen the glory of the coming of the Lord . . . ," Julia Ward Howe's "Battle Hymn of the Republic." No longer.

And even though the American Religion is a deep and important religion, it has generated remarkably little theological or devotional literature. It never had to; its doctrines and its concise sacred canon were well known.

All that has changed.

This book is an attempt to plug a hole in a levee, a hole where ignorance comes booming through, threatening to drown U.S. society. I attempt to plug this hole by saying plainly what the American Religion is and how it came to be. Of course no one book can do the job; we need thousands, and much else besides.

★　★　★

I have talked about belief in America, love of America—the American Religion. But we need to glance at America-hatred too. The distorted mirror of hatred can show us the truth, if we look carefully.

Other nationalisms have seemed threatening or hateful when they were *militarily* threatening or possibly when they tormented national minorities. But America has been hated by societies that had already gone over to American-style democracy; hated by nations that had nothing to fear from American power and knew it. America, Winston Churchill said during the Second World War, was the great republic "whose power arouses no fear and whose pre-eminence excites no jealousy."

Why is this sentiment no longer widely shared? What is *anti-*Americanism, and what accounts for its special ferocity?

Cut to the nation's capital, where the glittering elite's favorite activity is sneering. Ronald Reagan was great fun to sneer at. George W. Bush is even better; Reagan always produced among liberals a certain uneasy fear, because people *liked* him so much it was creepy—certain liberals were not wholly immune to his toxic charm themselves. But George W. shows no trace of the magic Reagan touch. Bush is no performer. He is merely a gritty, unglamorous President of the United States. Let's look at a report:

> At a dinner party in Washington, composed mainly of opponents of the war and the administration, [the president's policy was,] as usual with this class, the subject of vehement denunciation.

As usual. Washington dinner parties exist so that Republican presidents can be "vehemently denounced." But after a while, the report continues, a lone dissenter got up to say, in the president's defense, that "however deficient he may be in the head, he is all right in the heart." It's rare for anyone to defend a Republican president at a Washington dinner party—even to the extent of saying that he is okay as a person despite being stupid.

Anti-American sophisticates are positive that George W. is a semiamiable ignoramus *at best.* Most won't even be that generous.

But this particular Washington dinner party, with its lone presidential defender, took place during Abraham Lincoln's administration. I'm quoting from a book by the painter and Lincoln's friend F. B. Carpenter, published in 1866.

The writer and diplomat Henry Adams spent much of the Civil War in England. Adams wrote that, regarding Lincoln and his secretary of state William Seward, "English society seemed demented. Defence was useless; explanation was vain; one could only let the passion exhaust itself. One's best friends were as unreasonable as enemies, for the belief in poor Mr. Lincoln's brutality and Seward's ferocity became a dogma of popular faith."

But Abraham Lincoln was not "brutal." English society got it wrong. We may conclude at any rate that today's anti-Americanism has nothing to do with President George W. Bush, or the war in Iraq, or conservative judicial nominations, or any Republican policy whatsoever. It has been going on for a long time, with astonishingly little change in the big themes between 1863 and 2006.

Here's one more little scene. The United States (you will recall) was badly hurt on 9/11; it responded by launching military operations to sweep away the Taliban in Afghanistan and Saddam Hussein in Iraq. European and American liberals often speak of their sympathy for the oppressed. No peoples anywhere were better qualified as "oppressed" than Afghanis under the Taliban and Iraqis under Saddam. Liberals must have rejoiced to see America hosing those blood-drenched tyrannies down history's drain.

Yet in April 2003—after the Taliban had been beaten, soon after the Iraq war began—following a rally at an Ivy League college in favor of President Bush's policy (only four professors spoke, but the crowd was surprisingly large and enthusiastic)—one speaker was stopped by a colleague, who said: "Your speech was pretty good. But the fact is, it's getting awfully easy to hate this country."

Here at last was *America hatred*, naked and unashamed; out of the closet and proud! *"It's getting awfully easy to hate this country."* And the event that evidently brought this awareness about wasn't American support for some tinpot dictator, or an odious example of bigotry against blacks or women, or U.S. nonsupport for a worldwide environmental agreement, or a bloody-minded, uncivilized American refusal to allow U.S. officials to be hauled before the infallibly fair-minded judges at the International Court of Justice. No, the event that finally tipped the balance was . . . the rescue of the Iraqi people from Saddam Hussein.

Americanism must be powerful stuff indeed to provoke hatred of such exceptional, transparent purity. So *what is Americanism?*

★   ★   ★

I will tell the story of the emergence of Americanism in the form of a series of crucial American decisions taken by crucial American leaders at crucial moments. The Puritan exodus from Britain to the New World; the American Revolution; the Civil War; and America's decisions to enter World War I, to challenge the Soviets during the Cold War, to win the Cold War, and to fight Islamic terrorism.

Historians agree that Puritanism was dying by 1800; before long it disappeared entirely. But its influence reached deep into the twentieth century and beyond. During the 1600s Puritan leaders foresaw the city on a hill (John Winthrop), proclaimed the biblical mandate for democracy (Thomas Hooker), and introduced freedom of religion to the New World (Roger Williams). The preachers of the 1770s who urged Americans to support the Revolution were mostly Puritan or Puritan-inspired; a majority of the new nation's citizens were Puritan; many important founders and framers (John Adams, James Madison) had

Puritan backgrounds. Of course, many were not Puritan—some were Anglican like George Washington, or deist like Thomas Jefferson, or something else. But where Puritan influence fades, the Bible's influence usually remains strong—as it did for Washington and Jefferson. Abraham Lincoln was shaped by the Bible and by the plainest, most straightforward Protestant Christianity—which in turn was shaped by Puritanism.

In the twentieth century Woodrow Wilson took America into the First World War and proclaimed Americanism a world religion, which implied chivalrous duties abroad and at home. He read the Bible, prayed every day, and was shaped by his Presbyterian faith. Harry Truman, who led America into the Cold War and resurrected Wilson's activist, chivalrous Americanism, doted on the Bible. He read it seven times through during his White House years alone. Ronald Reagan, who announced that America must finally *win* the Cold War, was a devout Protestant; his Americanism might have been even more devout. Reagan reminded America of John Winthrop's prediction about a shining city on a hill. George W. Bush is a chivalrous American who believes in liberty, equality, and democracy not just for France and Denmark but for Arab nations where the residents have brown skin and strange ways. Our duty is to provide them too with liberty, equality, and democracy, says Bush. Most of my colleagues in academia don't disagree. They simply couldn't care less. They are too engrossed in hatred, of President Bush and his supporters and his America.

The Bible in English laid the basis of Puritanism—and of modern Britain, America, and the liberal democratic state. And the Bible posed a deep choice respecting the nature of war, which continues to occupy America and the world at large. So I will begin with the English Bible.

The American Religion has two basic components, a Creed and the doctrine I call American Zionism. Puritanism laid the basis of Americanism by developing American Zionism and other essential ingredients of the American Religion.

The revolutionary generation (influenced heavily by the Bible, Puritanism, and American Zionism) developed the American Creed, thereby completing the American Religion *in principle.* (I will discuss this in chapter 4.)

Then Abraham Lincoln and the Civil War (influenced heavily by the Bible, Puritanism, and the revolutionary generation) completed Americanism in practice by transforming American attitudes and American reality. Lincoln did more than anyone else to transform Puritanism into Americanism.

Woodrow Wilson was inspired by Americanism to take America into World War I—and to treat it as a war for American principles, not merely American interests. World War I created the world we inhabit today, the world to which modern Americanism belongs. Wilson believed that Americanism was a true global religion that imposed worldwide responsibilities on the American people. He believed that *we must act on American Zionism by spreading the Creed all over the world*—a view that remains intensely controversial today.

Finally, Americanism was a decisive influence on Truman at the start and Reagan at the end of the Cold War. Both presidents believed in an activist, Wilsonian, controversial Americanism. George W. Bush does too.

As I say, this is no history book and is not designed to present a balanced, objective look at the past. It is merely an essay intended to put right a drastic imbalance in our view of America and Americanism. If it slights one side of the argument (the secular, philosophical side), that is because the other side has been slighted so often for so many years. I am no Christian fundamentalist, but it doesn't take a fundamentalist to see that America could no more have grown up without Christianity and the Bible than a giant California redwood (or a human being) could have grown up without water and sunlight.

In short I will argue that . . .

America is not only a nation; America is a religious idea.

America is a biblical (not secular) republic. Americanism is a biblical (not civil) religion.

America and Americanism were shaped by Christianity, especially Puritan Christianity.

Puritan Christianity was shaped by the Bible, especially the Hebrew Bible.

The idea that liberty, equality, and democracy were ordained by God for all mankind, and that America is a new promised land richly blessed by and deeply indebted to God—that is Americanism.

Americanism is a biblical faith; it is also humane, in the best sense. You can believe in Americanism without believing in God—so long as you believe in man. You can pick these flowers, put them in water, admire their beauty. Just don't forget that they grew on a strong Judeo-Christian stem, rooted in the rich, deep soil of the Bible.

CHAPTER 2

THE WORLD-CREATING ENGLISH BIBLE

A merica started with the Puritans; the Puritans started with the Bible—specifically with the Bible translated into English. The English Bible is the most important book in British and American history by a wide margin. We take the English Bible for granted, but English itself is a fairly new language, and the idea of translating the original Hebrew and Aramaic of the Old Testament and Greek of the New into vernacular European languages was a controversial innovation of the late Middle Ages. So long as Latin translations were the only versions well known to Europe, access to the Bible could be controlled by the educated clergy and the cultural elite. The Bible was a radical book. Vernacular Bible translations, especially English ones, heralded the spread of Protestant Christianity, the rise of parliamentary power, the downfall of absolute monarchy, the onset of Puritanism—and the invention of America.

Scripture begins with God creating the world, but these verses don't tell you that the Bible has itself created worlds. Wherever you stand on the spectrum from devout to atheist, you must acknowledge that the Bible has been a creative force without parallel in human history.

The King James Bible, wrote the eminent British critic and author Sir Arthur Quiller-Couch in 1921, "has influenced our literature more deeply than any other book—more deeply even than all the writings of Shakespeare—far more deeply." The poet and painter William Blake called the Old and New Testaments "the Great Codes of Art." John Livingstone Lowe called the King James Bible "the noblest monument of English prose" (1936); George Saintsbury called it "probably the greatest prose work in any language" (1887). Nearly two millennia earlier the great Pharisee rabbi Hillel described the ideal life: "loving peace and pursuing peace; loving humanity and bringing it close to the Torah."

America's foremost prophet offered his own culminating vision in the Second Inaugural Address—"With malice toward none; with charity for all; with firmness in the right, as God gives us to see the right . . ." Many thinkers have noticed that this holiest document in the American canon is full of scriptural references and reads like an addendum to the Bible. This is significant for the nature of Americanism: it too is based on Scripture and is precisely an addendum to traditional Judaism and Christianity. It is an application of old principles to new problems.

You cannot study America or Americanism without encountering the Bible again and again. Americans who allow their bias against fundamentalists to prejudice them against the Bible itself make a foolish mistake. (Their bias against fundamentalists might also be a foolish mistake, but that's another question.) Those who take the Bible literally, on the other hand, are crazy if they fail to appreciate it as an artistic masterpiece too, of ineffable profundity, *and* as the most important book in British and American history.

Ronald Reagan called America "a great shining city on a hill," three and a half centuries after John Winthrop used the phrase while en route to Boston in 1630. Winthrop was invoking the famous verse in Matthew, "Ye are the light of the world. A city that is set on an hill cannot be hid" (5:14). These words hark back in turn to the prophets (Isa. 2:2–3, Mic. 4:2) and to the Book of Proverbs (4:18).

Here is a basic question about America that ought to be on page one of every history book: What made the nation's founders so sure they were on to something big? What made them so positive? Those first settlers and colonists, and the founding fathers, and all the generations that intervened before America did indeed emerge as a world power in the twentieth century: What made them so certain that America would become a light of the world, a shining city on a hill, a name fervently invoked by oppressed peoples all over the globe?

What made John Adams say in 1765 that "I always consider the settlement of America with reverence and wonder, as the opening of a grand scene and design in Providence"? What made Abraham Lincoln call America—in 1862, in the middle of a ruinous civil war—"the last, best hope of earth"?

We know of *people* who are certain of their destinies from childhood. But nations?

(America has not always lived up to its own principles. No nation ever has. But we have no right to allow this fact to blind us to the beauty of the American idea.)

Many things made all these Americans and proto-Americans sure that they were on to something good. And to some extent they were merely guessing and hoping. But one thing above all made them true prophets: they read the Bible. Winthrop, Adams, Lincoln, and thousands of others found a good destiny in the Bible and made it their own. They read about Israel's covenant with God and took it to heart: *they* were Israel. ("Wee are entered into Covenant with him for this worke," wrote Winthrop about the Lord. "Wee shall finde that the God of Israell is among us.") They read about God's chosen people and took it to heart: *they* were God's chosen people (or "*almost* chosen," as Lincoln put it). The Bible as they interpreted it told them what they could be and *would* be. Unless we understand the English Bible, where it came from and what it did, American history is a closed book in a strange tongue.

★ ★ ★

America's history starts with the emergence of Puritanism in sixteenth-century Britain. The Bible was central to the founding and development of Puritanism. The Bible's and Puritanism's histories are intermixed and impossible to separate completely. I will concentrate on the Bible here and on Puritanism in the next chapter.

The Bible is of course no single integrated work; it's a whole library of two Testaments (and the Apocrypha), each made of many books, each book with its own complex history. The New Testament is in some ways a continuation of Old Testament themes. But in others the New and Old Testaments are clearly different. In *these* areas Americans, reflecting Puritan practice, have often shown a surprising sympathy for the Old Testament view.

This is especially important in the field of war and peace. Many assume nowadays that there are two ways to look at war: pro or con, for or against, warmonger or pacifist. Americans have traditionally rejected this naïve dichotomy and insisted on a third alternative that grows straight out of the Hebrew Bible—and continues to get them into trouble when they explain their thinking to Europeans. This third view is chivalry, a far more serious topic than it's usually taken for; I return to it later.

The Emergence of the English Bible

The invention of printing in the mid-fifteenth century and the Protestant Reformation in the early sixteenth (whose central idea was that Scripture, not theologians, must impart Christianity to Christians) created an English Bible—reading craze. The masses were hungry for literature. Religion was the hottest topic on the agenda. Already in Henry VIII's reign (1509–47) the Bible was "disputed, rhymed, sung and jangled in every alehouse and tavern," according to the king himself—who was not happy about it. The Bible was a radical, subversive book.

Translating the Bible into English was no mere literary act: it was a controversial theological declaration. Religious reformers saw the English Bible as nothing less than a direct connection between ordinary Christian believers and the Lord. Translating the Scripture into English was sacred work; some were willing to die for it. They were opposed by such Roman Catholic stalwarts as Sir Thomas More, who expressed a widely held view when he proclaimed it "pestilential heresy" to think that "we should believe nothing but plain Scripture."*

The English Bible as we know it begins with John Wycliffe's

---

*Judaism agrees. For normative or Orthodox Jews, the Bible is only the starting point of a continuing discussion, led by the rabbis and learned teachers of the community. The only rational way for such Jews to read the Bible is through the lens of three thousand years of study and thought, starting with the Talmud and other rabbinic classics. For them the Bible *itself* develops, as a strange photographic negative might, from one state to a second, third, and endlessly onward as each generation applies its own characteristic developer. Our ancient forefathers were closer to God than we are, but after three thousand years of mulling, *we* are closer to God's law and God's truth—which in any case must change as life changes. The view of those Protestants who saw the Bible as a guide to work in the late fourteenth century. Wycliffe preached the primacy of the Bible and founded the Lollard movement, which in many ways looks forward to the Protestant Reformation.

When Wycliffe died in 1384, his English Bible was nearly complete. But his translation was banned in 1408, and the Lollards (who had become revolutionaries of a sort) were brutally suppressed. Many were burned alive with Bibles hung around their necks.

In the early sixteenth century the next great English translator, William Tyndale, announced to a learned theologian that "ere many years I will cause a boy that driveth the plough to know more of the scripture than thou dost." Tyndale was inspired by Martin Luther and dedicated to the task of producing an up-to-date English Bible. The English church denounced him; he fled to the Continent. He was declared a heretic anyway, arrested near Brussels, and executed in 1536.

Henry VIII banned Tyndale's translation for its alleged Protestant tendencies, but he promised the nation a religiously acceptable English Bible. Meanwhile he brought Protestantism to England in his own idiosyncratic way. From Henry's time onward the English Bible was an established fact of English life.

Queen Elizabeth I, England's favorite monarch, was Henry VIII's daughter. "No greater moral change ever passed over a nation than passed over England during the years which parted the middle of the reign of Elizabeth," wrote the historian John Richard Green in a famous passage (1874). "England became

---

living—a practical handbook that never needs revision—resembled an ancient Jewish heresy called Karaism but was otherwise basically new to history.

the people of a book, and that book was the Bible." Religious reformers, inspired by continental Protestants and the Bible itself, were unhappy with the Church of England, the "established church" that was closely associated with the monarchy. They wanted a biblical, *purified* Christianity. People called them Puritans.

Puritan is a confusing term. Puritanism was a *way of approaching* Protestant Christianity, not a church or denomination in its own right. Christians with Puritan inclinations were found in many different sorts of Protestant church—mainly in Congregationalist and Presbyterian churches but also in Anglican (or Episcopalian or Church of England) churches, Baptist churches, Quaker churches, and others too.

Naturally the Puritans, who were obsessed with the Bible, played an important role in the history of English Bible translations. The Geneva Bible, produced by English-speaking Protestants in the Swiss city, became and remained the Puritans' favorite. It had marginal notes that Puritans liked—but that King James and the Church of England deemed obnoxious. They were antimonarchy and pro-republic—"untrue, seditious, and savouring too much of dangerous and traitorous conceits," said the king. Under his sponsorship a new Bible was prepared (without interpretive notes) by forty-seven of the best scholars in the land. The King James Version appeared in 1611, intended merely as a modest improvement over previous translations. But it just happened to be a literary masterpiece of stupendous proportions. Purely on artistic grounds it ranks with Homer, Dante, and Shakespeare—Western literature's greatest achievements. In terms of influence and importance, it flattens those other three.

In the sixteenth and seventeenth centuries, the Bible was central to Britain's spiritual *and* intellectual life. The great historian of Britain G. M. Trevelyan wrote in 1926 that the advent of widely available English Bibles had a larger effect on English culture than any literary movement in England's history. Its effect was larger, in fact, than any *religious* movement's since the arrival of Christianity in Britain.

So we aren't discussing a merely popular or influential book. In sixteenth- and seventeenth-century Britain the English Bible was capable of affecting the first thoughts people had on waking, their last thoughts before falling asleep, and their dreams and nightmares. British homes were decorated with Bible quotations and Bible pictures painted or papered on the walls or printed on cloth wall-hangings. British life grew and flourished on a biblical trellis. Centuries later Quiller-Couch wrote of the Bible in Britain that "it is in everything we see, hear, feel, because it is in us, in our blood."

Friction between Puritans and the Church of England was an important cause of the English Civil War (1642–51)—which in turn was a major shaping event of the modern world. Parliament and the Puritans, to strip things down to essentials, rebelled against King Charles I and the Church of England. The Bible figured heavily on both sides, but especially among Puritans. The Puritan army was famous for chanting psalms. The Puritan leader Oliver Cromwell once halted his army during a hot pursuit so the soldiers could all chant Psalm 117 together. (He was a fine general; 117 is a short psalm.) The biblical passage in which Samuel warns the Israelites of the dangers of kingship was a natural Puritan favorite. But the Bible was important across the theological and political spectrum, to conservative Anglicans as well as to radical Puritans.

Modern scholars (such as Fania Oz-Salzberger, John Jacobs, and many others) have documented the Old Testament's influence on such seminal British Enlightenment and pre-Enlightenment thinkers as John Selden, Thomas Hobbes, and John Locke. They all agreed that ancient Israel built a nearly perfect republic lasting from the Exodus until the coronation of Israel's first king. This Israelite republic was a divinely designed state dedicated to liberty and social justice. Many thinkers held that this ancient republic was *the* perfect model for modern states to emulate.

John Locke is often said to be the most important philosophical influence on the American Revolution. Locke described a "social contract" in which citizens trade away some freedom in return for a civilized life: everyone's freedom is curtailed, and everyone benefits as well. The results are civil society and the state. The Bible was important to Locke's writing. Whenever he based his arguments on history and human experience, the Bible was his main source.

After the 1600s the Bible declined as a political issue in England, but much evidence attests to England's continuing habit of seeing itself as ancient Israel reborn—with an exalted destiny and special relationship to the Almighty. In 1719 Isaac Watts published a best-selling translation of the Psalms, in which references to "Israel" were replaced by the words "Great Britain." When the eminent German composer Georg Friedrich Händel settled in London, he determined, naturally, to do things British style. Thus he wrote a long series of oratorios—*Esther, Deborah, Judas Maccabaeus, Joshua, Susannah, Jephtha, Israel in Egypt*—all presupposing that Britain saw herself as the new Israel.

The Bible's influence on English literature was profound.

The work of John Milton, peerless Puritan poet and political agitator, would have been inconceivable without it—"that book within whose sacred context all wisdom is enfolded," Milton called it in 1642. Wordsworth said of Milton's poetry, "However imbued the surface might be with classical literature, he was a Hebrew in soul; all things tended in him towards the sublime." (The first-century Greek called Pseudo-Longinus got this ball rolling when he famously asserted that "sublimity" was the special characteristic of the Hebrew scriptures.)

The Bible continued to exert a vital influence on English literature through William Blake and the Romantics and down to our own day. In the literature of ancient Greece, Samuel Taylor Coleridge wrote, "all natural objects were *dead*, mere hollow statues," whereas "in the Hebrew poets each thing has a life of its own." In the Bible "I have found," he wrote, "words for my inmost thoughts, songs for my joy, utterances for my hidden griefs." In some of Lord Byron's *Hebrew Melodies*, poems to be sung to Hebrew tunes, the poet captured the mood and the matter of the biblical Song of Songs: "She walks in beauty, like the night / Of cloudless climes and starry skies; / And all that's best of dark and bright / Meet in her aspect and her eyes." There are countless more examples of the Bible's centrality to English literature.

The English Bible in America

America's earliest settlers came in search of religious freedom, to escape religious persecution—important facts that Americans sometimes forget. A new arrival who joined the Pilgrims at Plymouth in 1623 "blessed God for the opportunity of freedom and liberty to enjoy the ordinances of God in purity among His people." It is a perfect reflection of the nation's origins that the very first freedom named in the Bill of Rights—Article I, part one—should be religious freedom.

You cannot understand the literature and experience of seventeenth-century American Puritans unless you know the Bible. There is a fascinating resemblance between Puritan writings and the Hebrew literary form called *melitzah*, in which the author makes his point by stringing together biblical and rabbinic passages. The Puritans' world, like traditional Jewish society, was permeated by and obsessed with the Bible.

Enemies of America and Britain have long suspected the existence of an Anglo-Saxon conspiracy to rule the world; this paranoid suspicion arose long before the Iraq war. It might have had something to do with the Bible-centered cultural history that the two nations share. They speak of a "special relationship" with each other—but each also has a history of believing in its own "special relationship" with the Lord Himself.

People have reached no agreement on whether God created the world, but the Bible's awe-striking creative powers are undeniable. People disagree on whether God "is not a man that He should lie" (Num. 23:19), but the Hebrew Bible's uncanny honesty respecting Israel and its many sins is plain. The faithful ask, in the words of the 139th Psalm, "Whither shall I go from Thy spirit? or whither shall I flee from Thy presence?" And answer, "If I take the wings of the morning, and dwell in the uttermost parts of the sea; Even there shall Thy hand lead me, and Thy right hand shall hold me." Secularists don't see it that way, but the Bible's penetration into the farthest corners of

the known world is simple fact. Most contemporary philosophers and culture critics are barely aware of these things; they
don't see the pattern behind them, can't tell us what the pattern
means, and for the most part don't care.

But America and Americanism are both impenetrable unless
we start with the Bible.

America's Puritans were Christians who believed absolutely
in the divinity of Jesus. But they were also obsessed with their
role as the "new chosen people" in the "new promised land,"
and they were fascinated with the Hebrew Bible. The Puritans
set the tone for many aspects of American Christianity. They
have much to do with the fact that American-style Christianity
is "Old Testament Christianity"—a phrase Robert Frost used
to describe his own religious views.

Old Testament Christianity recognizes the sanctity of the
New Testament and rates it higher than the Hebrew Bible's;
Old Testament Christians are thoroughly Christian, not at all
Jewish. But they often seem to think of the Old Testament be-
fore the New, and to see things, as the Puritans did, from the
Hebrew Bible's standpoint. Partly this reflects the characteris-
tic American preference for "peace through strength" and
"democratic chivalry," which the Hebrew Bible endorses, over
the pacifism preached by some verses of the New Testament.
But there is more to America's Old Testament predilection.
America has seen herself from the start as the "New American
Israel."

Not surprisingly, Old Testament Christianity was popular in
the Puritan 1600s. And the era of the Revolution used the biblical Exodus as a model for America's own rebellion against
tyranny. But Abraham Lincoln ("spiritual center of American

---

history," as the historian Sidney Mead called him) gave us our clearest look at Old Testament Christianity.

Lincoln was asked many times why he refused to join a church, although he believed profoundly in a personal God. The plainest answer on record (which resembles other statements he made at other times) is the one he gave Congressman Henry C. Deming of Connecticut: "When any church will inscribe over its altar as its sole qualification for membership the Savior's condensed statement of the substance of both the law and the Gospel, Thou shalt love the Lord thy God with all thy heart, and with all thy soul, and with all thy mind, and thy neighbor as thyself,—that Church will I join with all my heart and soul." (This "condensed statement" appears in Luke 10:25–27 and Matthew 22:36–40.) Lincoln was citing indirectly, just as Jesus himself did, two verses of the Hebrew Bible, from Leviticus and Deuteronomy. Lincoln put Jesus right at the center of his spiritual life—yet derived its *substance* from the Hebrew Bible. This is a perfect picture of Old Testament Christianity.

Roughly two hundred years ago Edmund Burke famously wrote, "The age of chivalry is gone: that of sophisters, economists and calculators has succeeded: and the glory of Europe is extinguished for ever."

Chivalry is essentially a religious idea; a Judeo-Christian idea; a biblical idea. Old Testament attitudes toward war are central to the history of chivalry. And chivalry is important to America. What should we call the heroism of America's combat troops in Iraq, who fight bravely every day for the weak against the strong, if not *chivalrous*?

In the late 1200s the Spaniard Ramon Llull wrote a handbook of chivalry that required aspirants to "protect the weak,

women, widows and orphans"; it required that a knight "be
ready to go out from his castle to defend the ways and to pursue robbers and malefactors." In other words, knights were to
make the world safe for decent people. In a treatise of around
1350 the Frenchman Geoffrey de Charny wrote that "those
who have served with distinction in wars in their own land are
to be honoured, but still more to be honoured are those who
have seen service in distant and strange countries."

Even though chivalry was a *Christian* duty, its underpin-
nings lay in classical Israel—which in time made chivalry a
perfect fit to American thinking. Christian scholars developed
theories of just war, but the New Testament provides no model
of what an ethical, God-fearing warrior is supposed to be. The
Old Testament does.

Even before the word *chivalry* came into use, early European
ceremonies for blessing swords and banners cited the brave,
godly warriors of the Hebrew Bible. Galahad of the Arthur stories was said to be King David's descendant. By the late twelfth
century French translations of individual biblical books already circulated; Judges and Kings, with their stories of heroic
warriors, were among the favorites.

The apocryphal books of the Maccabees were particularly
important, especially where they focus on Judah Maccabee,
hero of the Hanukkah story, who led a successful Israelite rebellion against Hellenistic tyrants. In one medieval chronicle
Charlemagne laments his comrade Roland as the veritable peer
of Judah Maccabee—and dedicates twelve thousand ounces of
gold and the same of silver to the memory of those who died at
the great battle of Roncesvalles, "and in remembrance of the
Maccabees." "For the perfect model of knighthood," de Charny
wrote, "one should look to Judas Maccabaeus."

And what *are* the Hebrew Prophets, after all, but recruiters for proto–knights in arms to protect widows and orphans, feed the hungry, shelter the homeless, and above all free the captive all over the world—while cleansing and purifying the service of the Lord?

America took up this same large theme of chivalry. But American chivalry, unlike Europe's, had nothing to do with aristocracy. Americans and colonial settlers believed that it was their Christian (or Judeo-Christian) duty to intervene on the side of right. The great essayist E. B. White once gave a perfect definition of democratic chivalry: "To meddle in other people's affairs frequently, gallantly, and without warning—but with no ulterior motive."

Americans started lecturing the world on right and wrong long before the United States was born. (That's one reason the world loves us so much.) Lincoln looked at war not only as a means of self-protection but as an instrument of God's justice. If God willed the Civil War to continue, said Lincoln, until the sin of slavery was expiated by the blood and treasure of South *and* North, "as was said three thousand years ago so still it must be said: The judgments of the Lord are true and righteous altogether" (Ps. 19:9). Woodrow Wilson turned Lincoln's worldview outward. Today in Iraq the American nation is struggling to digest the new dangers, opportunities, and chivalrous duties of the post–Cold War world.

I will mention democratic chivalry frequently in this book. The reason Americans once fought in a world war to make the world safe for democracy—then propped up the legitimate governments of Greece and Turkey against communist threats and thereby joined the Cold War—is *democratic chivalry*. The reason President Bush proposes to go forth and knock down

tyrants all over the world is *democratic chivalry*. But whenever
you hear the phrase *democratic chivalry*, think "American
Zionism." Aristocrats in medieval Europe controlled a vast poor
peasant society; chivalry helped them ease their consciences.
They *deserved* their exalted positions, they told themselves, on
account of their good behavior. But America rejected aristocracy from the very first. So why should Americans be chivalrous? Because of American Zionism.

They were a new chosen people in a new promised land,
blessed far beyond their deserts. They were grateful to God and
indebted to God. They owed Him. Americans took up chivalry
to pay a debt to the Lord—and to reassure themselves that they
too *deserved* their blessings on account of good behavior. Looking back on the Puritan settlements created during the first
part of the seventeenth century, the Pilgrim father William
Bradford associated their evident success (blessings received
from the Lord) with their usefulness (blessings chivalrously returned to the wider community). "Thus out of small beginnings," he wrote, "greater things have been produced by His
hand that made all things out of nothing . . . ; and as one small
candle may light a thousand; so the light here kindled hath
shown unto many, yea, in some sort, to our whole nation." The
settlements succeeded; the whole nation was illuminated.
Blessings were received, and blessings were returned. That is
democratic chivalry. Eventually it took a far more active form.

Chivalry and not secularism inheres in the idea of America—but it is chivalry with an American twist. This chivalry is a
profoundly serious *religious* ideal—a Judeo-Christian idea—a
biblical idea.

And if there is one all-important missing ingredient in
American intellectuals' (and many young people's) worldview

today, it is chivalry in the largest sense. Many of my academic colleagues seem unable to grasp that young U.S. soldiers might *want* to be in Iraq, might *want* to face the enemy in combat, might *hope to use* their strong arms on behalf of the suffering. Valor and honor, bravery and heroism in a godly cause—most American intellectuals draw a blank when you mention these things. They don't understand, and they know they don't. And sometimes they are proud they don't.

In some parts of this nation we have reared a generation of young people to whom chivalry is equally incomprehensible. You can read their confusion in large gestures and small. Too many young people are oblivious to the idea that Iraqis under Saddam were a tortured, suffering people who desperately needed our help and are deeply grateful—polls show—that our soldiers generously, bravely, and heroically gave it.

Too many young men are utterly unchivalrous in a different sense, in their approach to young women. The girls, however they are treated, will give the boys what they want (one young man told me recently)—so why should the boys put themselves out?

But America remains chivalry's stronghold. Chivalry, like Puritanism, is biblical in origin. And America remains the biblical republic.

CHAPTER 3

AMERICAN ZIONISM

The Puritan Dream of America

The Puritans who settled the eastern seaboard of the future United States fathered the nation we are today. To understand America and Americanism, you must understand those Puritans. They are a difficult proposition, an intellectual handful. They were religious fanatics. But their intolerance gave birth to toleration; their quest for religious freedom yielded freedom in general; and their devotion to the Bible and the biblical idea of covenant contributed significantly to the modern liberal state. In many ways we remain the nation they wanted us to be.

Puritans wished to be as close to God as human beings can. The flame of Puritan devotion burned so hot, bright, brilliant, and pure that it burned itself out in a couple of centuries; today there are no Puritans left. In the end they were forced to blend quietly into the Protestant world like a great roaring, crashing breaker reduced to a sheet of gleaming foam, sliding tamely back to sea. But they left behind powerful, permanent changes. The modern world was fired in the kiln of red-hot Puritan religious genius.

It's easy to see how deeply Puritanism marked America. Many Americans still think their nation is blessed, has a mission from God, and must aspire to the very highest ideals. Many are still deeply religious and attached to the Bible. Many still have the Puritans' taste in religion: straight up and undiluted; simple, strong, and direct, with a marked sympathy for the Old Testament. And many still believe what John Winthrop wrote in 1630: "Wee shall be as a Citty upon a Hill, the eies of all people are upon us."*

The culture war that has split this country since the late 1960s is largely a war over America's Puritan legacy. Do we live with it or against it? The argument continues. The fighting is fierce. But how did a religious doctrine come to be so important for America and the world?

Puritanism inspired intrepid Britons to set out for the New World, for their own promised land. Puritans knew from the start that their mission and self-assurance would seem arrogant. John Winthrop's group consisted of four hundred men, women, and children bound for Massachusetts Bay on four ships. Before setting out, they published a statement from aboard ship announcing that they did *not* regard themselves as holier than other men. We "cannot part from our native Coun-

---

*Some of my quotations from Puritan writings in this chapter use the original spellings, and some don't. I prefer the old spellings, which are rarely hard to make out and remind us that we are looking across a four-hundred-year gap. But some modern editors and historians have chosen to substitute modern spellings, and when I cite their versions, I use their spellings.

try," they added, "without much sadness of heart, and many teares in our eyes." These are not the words of angry self-righteousness.

Their Puritan faith sustained the early settlers through cruelly hard ocean voyages, tough and deadly early winters, and all the trials of life in an unknown, unmapped region at the outer edge of the civilized world. Those settlers played a crucial role in fashioning the earliest version of Americanism, creating it out of ideas developed at the ragged edge of Western civilization. They invented American Zionism and started to weave the American Creed on a great biblical loom. (They left the Creed unfinished, but the revolutionary generation completed it.) They bequeathed to us many of the qualities that make America great and many of the ones that make people hate us. Often those are one and the same.

Given its decisive importance in creating modern America (*and* Britain, to a lesser extent), Puritanism ranks with the half-dozen decisive forces in the shaping of the modern world. Of these, it is probably the least understood. Hatred of Puritanism is one of the best-established bigotries of modern times. *Puritan* has been an insult for hundreds of years. It suggests rigidity, austerity, censoriousness—exactly the kind of religion secularists love to hate. Puritans *were* rigid and censorious, up to a point; most stereotypes are partly true. But they were much else besides.

Puritanism was a British invention, but American Puritanism differed in important ways from its parent. American Puritans ran their communities on the basis of exclusivity: civil rights belonged only to those with sound religious views. Puritans did *not* build "theocracies"—most of their communities were run by laymen, not preachers. Yet American Puritans took for granted that civil authority should operate in accordance with God's law as set forth in the Bible.

Most Puritan settlements tolerated only one type of church—ordinarily Congregationalist or Presbyterian. In some communities the whole population had to attend services, but church *membership* was restricted to a minority of "visible saints"—who could give convincing public accounts of the entry of God's "saving grace" into their lives. This purest-of-all Puritan doctrines, with its sharp restrictions on church membership, was known as "the New England Way." Many Old English Puritans back home disapproved. In any case, the New England Way got impossibly tangled up in practical difficulties, and the purists had to backpedal. In larger terms, this is the story of Puritanism as a whole.

But American Puritans were intensely creative too. Some discovered the equality of man in their Bibles. Pondering their Bibles and the structure of English corporations, they invented a primitive but serviceable type of democracy. And they invented a form of Christianity that worked with and not against the grain of human life. Partly for that reason Americans remain to this day more at peace than any other Western people with the Bible and Christianity.

For all their passionate rigidity, America's seventeenth-century Puritan leaders were above all religious seekers, hoping to worship God with their whole lives, body and soul, with a dazzling fervor that still lights up their journals, letters, and poetry three hundred years later.

"That man is in a lethargy," wrote the New England preacher Nathaniel Ward in 1645, "who does not sensibly feel God shaking the heavens over his head and the earth underneath his feet." In the early eighteenth century the great theologian Jonathan Edwards wrote of being "wrapped and swallowed up in God." "The Puritans wanted that fullness of life that made David dance before the ark," wrote the historian J. D. Dow in 1897. Puritanism was the eruption of a volcanically powerful desire to know God and do His will.

Edward Taylor was a distinguished Puritan poet whose work lay undiscovered until 1937. He was born in England, came to America, graduated from Harvard in 1671, and became a minister. His "meditations," addressed to the Lord, reveal the Puritan soul:

Oh! that my love might overflow my heart
To fire the same with love! For love I would.
But oh! My streight'ned Breast! My Lifeless Sparke!
My Fireless Flame! What Chilly Love, and Cold?
In measure small! In Manner Chill! See!
Lord, blow the Coal: Thy Love Enflame in mee.

America was born out of such (awkward, groping, intensely felt, overwhelmingly vivid) love poetry to God.*

---

*Thomas H. Johnson, ed., *The Poetical Works of Edward Taylor* (Princeton, N.J.: Princeton University Press, 1939). Quotations of Puritan writings in this chapter are drawn mainly from Samuel Eliot Morison, ed., *Of Plymouth Plantation 1620–1647 by William Bradford* (New York: Alfred A. Knopf, 1970); James Kendall Hosmer, ed., *Winthrop's Journal, 1630–1649* (New York: Charles Scribner's Sons, 1908): Cotton Mather, *Magnalia Christi Americana; or, The Ecclesiastical History of New-England* (Hartford, Conn.: Silas Andrus and Son, 1855), reprint of the original 1702 edition; Cotton Mather, *Essays to Do Good, Addressed to All Christians, whether in Publick*

In one of Shakespeare's most famous images, Macbeth imagines—in a panic, after murdering his king—that plunging his bloodstained hand in the ocean would turn the whole sea red. The Puritans actually *had* that supernormal intensity. They have dyed four hundred years of history—although by the nineteenth century they had all but used themselves up, burned themselves out, and disappeared. They changed the world, then faded like stars at daybreak.

To understand Puritanism, we must understand its incandescent, subversive genius. In this chapter I will summarize the rise of Puritanism, then discuss the wide-ranging, surprising Puritan contribution to America's personality. I will turn finally to the development of American Zionism and the Puritans' preliminary ideas on the topics of the American Creed—liberty, equality, democracy.

The Rise of Puritanism

In the early 1500s Martin Luther kicked off the Reformation by inventing Protestant Christianity. He was ashamed of the corruption and lax luxury of the medieval church. He saw the

---

or *Private Capacities* (Dover, Mass.: Samuel C. Stevens, 1826), reprint of the original 1710 edition; Perry Miller, ed., *The American Puritans: Their Prose and Poetry* (Garden City, N.Y.: Doubleday Anchor Books, 1956); and Alexander Young, ed., *Chronicles of the Pilgrim Fathers of the Colony of Plymouth from 1602 to 1625* (Boston: Charles C. Little and James Brown, 1841). I've also drawn on Edmund S. Morgan, *Visible Saints: The History of a Puritan Idea* (Ithaca, N.Y.: Cornell University Press, 1963) and other books by Morgan; on Sydney E. Ahlstrom's magisterial and indispensable *A Religious History of the American People* (New Haven, Conn.: Yale University Press, 1972); and others.

church as a decadent, complicated mess. He wanted to sweep away the gigantic, ramifying bureaucracy that separated Christians from the Lord. Priests, bishops, archbishops, cardinals, and popes all had to go. Likewise the many monastic orders with their abbots and priors and enormous bureaucracies, and the cults of saints and relics, and the cults of the Virgin, and all heavenly intermediaries, deal-makers, and go-betweens: all must be swept away.

"Every Christian a priest," Luther taught. Each Christian had a personal responsibility to read and understand the Bible.

Luther's teachings had big consequences for England. England's reaction to Luther was very different from Germany's. (In Germany the Reformation inspired peasant revolts that were ruthlessly suppressed—with Luther's approval. Some German states became officially Protestant; others stayed Catholic. The split survived for centuries.)

King Henry VIII brought the Reformation to England in a fit of pique. He had been a good Catholic to start out. In fact, he had published a tract against Luther that was commended by the pope. But he wanted to get rid of his first wife so he could marry Anne Boleyn. He desired a male heir, and his first wife had failed to produce one.

In the early sixteenth century getting rid of your wife was a ticklish business, even for a king. The pope refused to annul Henry's marriage. So Henry cut England's connections with the Church of Rome and resolved to take care of English souls all by himself. But he was no true Protestant in Luther's sense. His goal was to seize control of the English church, then squeeze the monasteries dry and abolish them, not to reform English Christianity.

After Henry came a short-lived child king (Edward VI) with Protestant-leaning advisors, then a strong-minded Catholic queen. Bloody Mary (she reigned till 1558) did her best to return England to the Catholic camp; she burned nearly three hundred Protestants to make her intentions plain. No one doubted her sincerity. But these brutal, beastly persecutions blew up in her face: they created a disgust with Catholicism that lingered for centuries, and they helped convince large numbers of Englishmen that they ought to be Protestants.

During Mary's reign, many reform-minded Christians fled to Protestant centers on the Continent—especially to Geneva, where John Calvin's rigorously "pure" Protestantism appealed to English exiles and where an annotated English translation called the Geneva Bible took shape. Calvin was to be a major influence on Puritanism. His teachings helped make Puritanism uncompromising and, in the view of many non-Puritans, forbidding. But Calvin's influence also paved the way for English and (even more) American affection for the Old Testament; for English and (far more) American resistance to anti-Semitism. "Centuries of Christian blood libels against the nation of Israel were suddenly countered by Calvinist theology."*

Mary was succeeded by Elizabeth, Anne Boleyn's daughter and England's favorite monarch. Elizabeth settled the religious question forever, she thought, by establishing the Church of England in 1559. (But no religious question ever has been settled forever.)

---

*Armand Laferrère, "The Huguenots, the Jews, and Me," *Azure*, Autumn 2006, p. 73. Catholics and most Protestants taught that Christianity rendered Judaism obsolete; Calvin taught that the Jewish religion was and remained a sign of God's special love for the Jewish people.

The Church of England was a compromise. Most Roman Catholics could not accept it. Many Protestants couldn't either; the Puritans demanded a purified church. But most Puritans who sailed to America in the early days insisted that they had *not* renounced the Church of England. They were sure they could build better, holier communities than the ones they were leaving behind, but they were not "separationists"; they did not denounce the Anglican church.

Puritanism is a complex worldview. One way to glimpse its overall structure is to start at the top: Puritans hope to live as close as they can to God. ("Oh! that my love might overflow my heart.") Two points follow.

First, they must read and know the Bible. Puritans are sure that the Bible is mankind's one guaranteed connection with God. They reject the idea of modern-day prophecy, of direct revelation from God to man in the postbiblical era.

Second, Puritanism must be *simple* and must sweep away all artificial, corrupt, and impure embellishments of Christianity and Christian worship and all intermediaries between God and man. Puritans aimed to abolish the Roman Catholic–style hierarchy that was part of Anglicanism, and the prayer book, and clerical vestments, and elaborate church services. For Puritans, the sermon was the main event. Laymen dealt directly with the Bible; ministers spoke directly to their congregations.

The doctrine of predestination preached by John Calvin was central to Puritans. It may be the one aspect of Puritanism that is hardest for moderns to sympathize with. Puritans reasoned that, because of Adam's sin and the fall of man, men were born sinful, able to control their behavior but not their thoughts. Even good men sinned in their hearts. They simply couldn't help it. After the fall, man was incapable of reaching heaven on his own power.

But the Passion of Jesus—the Lord's son, one person of the Trinity—created a pool of grace. God could bestow grace from this pool on unworthy human beings in a sort of spiritual baptism. Preselected ("predestined") unworthies (*all* men were unworthy) were saved and would go to heaven. God's choices had no discernible relationship to human behavior; in any case, a man's destiny was decided before he was born. Certain human beings were predestined for salvation; the rest were worthy only of damnation. This hard, uncompromising faith tried to push Christianity to its logical conclusions and live honestly with the result.

Which could be heartless. In Boston a young girl drowned in a well. Her father admitted that he had profaned the Lord's Sabbath—and the Puritan sense of justice was satisfied. (At least *some* Puritans were satisfied.) "Some very judicious persons have observed," wrote the eminent preacher Cotton Mather, smugly, that "as they sanctify the Lord's day, remissly or carefully, just so their affairs usually prospered all the ensuing week."

People who were chosen would know it; they would experience the entrance of God's grace into their lives. All Christians had to obey God's will, in order to be worthy of grace should they be selected. A Christian who was destined for saving grace would first experience "saving faith." The saved came only from the ranks of the perfectly faithful; perfect faith, in turn, could come only from God. Here Puritans relied on a story that ranked for them, as for the Jews, among the most important in the Bible. God makes a covenant with Abraham that can never be abrogated; it will last forever. The text says of Abraham, "And he believed in the Lord, Who accounted it to him for righteousness" (Gen. 15:6). Abraham's faith made him *worthy* of the covenant.

Perry Miller, the eminent historian of Puritanism, wrote in 1953 that "the conception of a covenant was to certain English Puritans, above all to those who populated New England, the master idea of the age." Historians rarely commit themselves to such sweeping, imposing declarations—but when they do, we should listen. The Hebrew word *brith*—as in the organization B'nai B'rith, or the Jewish circumcision ceremony called a *bris*—became *covenant* in English, *foedus* in Latin. The Latin word gave birth to *federal* and *federalism*, words that became vital to American history.

Individuals could enter into a covenant with God, but whole communities could too. New England's Puritan settlements saw themselves as "covenant communities," bound as one to God. If they were faithful to the covenant and God's will, He would bless them. Otherwise He would punish them.

Marriage is a covenant too, and the *covenant with God* has a suggestive resonance with the idea of *marriage with God.* Israel's prophets heard it and sometimes said so explicitly. New England divines heard it too, and so did Puritan poets. "What! hath thy Godhead, as not satisfi'de, / Marri'de our Manhood, making it its Bride?" wrote Edward Taylor. Passion is always skirting forbidden territories.

But theological radicals are not necessarily political radicals.

Most Puritans did not want to fight the English monarchy and established church; they wanted to win them over *without* fighting. Some tried and failed to get Parliament to convert the Church of England into a Presbyterian church, ruled by boards of elders. But others wanted a "reformation without tarrying for any" and became "separatists," repudiating the Church of England and the whole idea of a centralized church. They insisted that each congregation should choose its own minister; no higher authority should appoint one.

Queen Elizabeth tolerated the Puritans. When she died and the Stuarts came to power, big political changes followed. When James I succeeded Elizabeth in 1603, the Puritans were a strong and growing force, just on the point of emerging as a major cultural and political power. James's ascension was an exciting development for Puritans—many believed that he favored Puritan ideas. But they were wrong. Before long he officially rejected Puritanism in favor of the Church of England. His new anti-Puritan policy was announced at the Hampton Court conference of 1604—which also gave birth to the King James Bible project. James proclaimed of the Puritans that "I shall make them conform themselves or I will harry them out of the land."

Thereby began a feud that lasted three generations and brought about the momentous English Civil War and, ultimately, the transfer of sovereign power from the king to the Commons.* Persecuted Puritans set sail in rising numbers for the New World

---

*Another permanent consequence was the tragic destruction by Protestant fanatics of medieval artworks that they deemed impious—especially sculpture and stained glass that depicted human beings, and shrines for the worship of saints. The first waves of destruction began under Henry VIII (who had a Commission for the Destruction of Shrines). Much survived, but much was lost forever to the fury of those who made it their business to attack "the abomynation of ydolatry" in the fifteenth and sixteenth centuries. Today Yale University still (subtly) proclaims its Puritan roots in the form of dozens of empty niches built into the facades of its imitation English Gothic buildings. The original empty niches are still to be found in England; they once held medieval statuary, smashed by fanatics and never replaced.

in search of religious freedom. Things got even worse for English Puritans under Charles I and Archbishop William Laud; Puritan emigration to America increased. By the mid-seventeenth century many Puritan settlements were solidly established in America, especially though not only in New England.

In 1609, five years after Hampton Court, a separatist congregation in an English town unpromisingly named Scrooby fled as a group to Leiden in Holland. They sought freedom to worship as Puritans without interference or harassment. In Holland they could worship as they pleased but found it hard to support themselves. And some did not want their children to live among non-English-speakers in a non-English society. Some worried that Holland might go to war and that they might be involved. So in 1619 one part of the congregation decided to go to America. They first returned to England, then set sail for the New World in two ships, *Speedwell* and *Mayflower*. But *Speedwell* proved unseaworthy, and after two attempted departures she limped back to port in disgrace.* So the Pilgrims all crowded together into the *Mayflower*. After a long, hard crossing, they landed on Cape Cod and then pushed on to Plymouth, where they arrived in December 1620.

Puritanism in America

Englishmen had first settled in America at Roanoke Island, Virginia, in 1585. That colony failed, and tried again, and

---

*See W. Sears Nickerson, *Land Ho!—1620: A Seaman's Story of the* Mayflower, *Her Construction, Her Navigation and Her First Landfall* (Boston: Houghton Mifflin, 1931).

failed again, and vanished. But the idea of colony-making survived.

In the early 1600s English settlers came for good. They founded Jamestown, Virginia, under the auspices of England's Virginia Company in 1607. The new settlement had a Puritan flavor and called itself a Puritan-style "covenant community." It succeeded because of tobacco; around 1613 Virginians began planting high-quality West Indian varieties.

By 1619 the Jamestown settlement was more than a thousand strong. By the 1620s Virginia was moving toward the Church of England and away from Puritanism.

In New England things were different. The Pilgrims, as I have mentioned, founded Plymouth Plantation in 1620. Eight years later the founding of the Massachusetts Bay Colony created another Puritan community. Boston was founded in 1630.

Plymouth Plantation was created by separatists who believed that the Church of England was terminally corrupt and that honest people had one choice only: to leave it and to clear out of England before God's wrath leveled the place like Sodom and Gomorrah. But the founders of Massachusetts Bay were *non*separatists and underlined that fact. Their duty, as they saw it, was to help England and the English church reform themselves and correct their faults, by setting up a model church and society for emulation.

But inevitably American Puritanism began diverging from the English variety. New England Puritans introduced a new twist on Puritan theology. Evidently it originated in 1635 or 1636, in Massachusetts Bay. Henceforth church membership would be restricted to those who gave convincing evidence that they had been chosen for salvation. Theologians had decided what evidence would be acceptable; certainty about God or your own fate was a sign that God had *not* chosen you. In the Puritan scheme, religious *doubt* and not perfect assurance was right, normal, and encouraging, in a sense even mandatory.

The New England Way turned Puritanism into a kind of performing art. Candidates for church membership had to tell their spiritual life-stories to the whole church membership— although you might be allowed to speak before a board of elders if you were uneasy about a larger audience. Thus New England developed a controversial test for church membership that centered on what I will call a *sacred narrative*. This development was significant because sacred narrative is a pregnant form in American spiritual history.

From John Winthrop to Martin Luther King, Jr., Americans have found it natural to narrate historical events with an eye to the Lord's role. The greatest practitioner of this art was Abraham Lincoln.

Sacred narrative was *the* characteristic literary form of ancient Israel too. Thus, one more point of contact between classical Israel and American Puritanism.

Massachusetts Bay was an early, distinctive American democracy, reflecting the influence of English commercial practices, among other things.

Most colonies (including Massachusetts) were operated by commercial businesses with their headquarters in England. But the Massachusetts Bay Company took the radical step of moving its headquarters from Europe to Massachusetts. The company directors would henceforth be actual *residents* of the colony. Back in England, the directors had chosen John Winthrop as governor. In Massachusetts, Winthrop decided that all freemen—

basically the whole adult male population—should vote for the company's officers and directors (who were also, ex officio, the *colony's* officers and directors).

The Puritans continued to create new institutions and new settlements. Harvard College dates from 1635, the colony of New Haven from 1638. (Harvard's first president and the co-founder of New Haven were brothers.) In 1639 emigrants from Massachusetts organized the settlement of Connecticut. Connecticut's first leader was the eminent preacher Thomas Hooker, who preferred more lenient church-membership tests than Massachusetts was using. New Haven, on the other hand, under the spiritual leadership of John Davenport, was all in favor of strict tests—the stricter the better. The New Haven Colony was absorbed by Connecticut in 1662. (Yale University wasn't born until 1701.)

Despite some disagreements, New England Puritans did their best to codify distinctive American beliefs and practices. In 1648 the Cambridge Platform was adopted by representatives of the four orthodox Puritan colonies of New England: Plymouth, Massachusetts Bay, Connecticut, and New Haven.

Roger Williams founded Rhode Island as an officially Puritan colony with a twist: religious liberty for non-Puritans. He had been expelled from Massachusetts for preaching a Puritanism that was too pure for the authorities to stomach. In Rhode Island he underwent a change of heart. William Penn's colony of Pennsylvania was officially Quaker, loosely associated with Puritanism. The Quakers (properly the Society of Friends) made the Puritan emphasis on simplicity the center of their worldview. Maryland was established by Roman Catholics but soon had a Puritan majority. New Jersey was established by former New Havenites who wanted to restore to Puritan practices their original strictness and purity.

Puritan influence was important in *every* British colony in the future United States—including the southern colonies that had moved officially into the Anglican camp. At independence in 1776 roughly three-quarters of American citizens and 85 percent of American churches were Puritan.

I've sketched Puritan doctrine briefly. But one aspect of Puritanism transcends doctrine and lives at the boundary between "practical philosophy" and aesthetics. It hasn't received the attention it deserves.

Puritans in England and America believed in the dignity and godliness of *simplicity*.

Simplicity as a worldview was especially important in America. Reinforced by the natural limitations of New World life far from European craftsmen, models, and materials, restrained simplicity emerged as *the* American style—an aesthetic with theological roots. It was a noble and dignified aesthetic, a transparent, "democratic" aesthetic (you didn't have to be rich to work, dress, or live in this style) of which Americans were quietly proud and in many cases still are.

In Europe the sheer profusion and gorgeousness of history's relics are mesmerizing. The extraordinary art, and the profoundly great buildings in towns and cities that are artworks in themselves on a colossal scale—all this brings any normal human being to a halt. Europeans sometimes become inured to great art. Americans don't have the same opportunity and don't face the corresponding danger.

Any American who compares a beautiful and profound medieval cathedral in Europe to a plain salt-white American church is apt to conclude that the American style is just as noble as the European, just as profound, and ultimately just as beautiful. But it is hard to overemphasize the plainness of those early colonial churches—or meetinghouses, as the Puritans called them. (*Meetinghouse* was the standard term until the 1770s; these buildings were used as churches *and* town halls.) Ordinarily the meetinghouse had no steeple, and its front was a square-ish rectangle topped by a triangle, like a child's drawing of a house—with tall windows and a modestly decorated door, clapboard siding, and a slate roof. Usually there was a graveyard nearby, and solid, simple wooden houses stood all around. The sea was on one side, dense woods on the other, and a narrow strip lay in between for building, planting, and pondering the Lord. Often those settlements had an austere and moving dignity, like old books in which each printed letter is sunk softly into the heavy page.

Simplicity was an attribute of American Puritan lawmaking too. In Massachusetts ten crimes were punishable by death, as the Hebrew Bible specifies: idolatry, witchcraft, blasphemy, murder, bestiality, sodomy, adultery, man-stealing, false witness, and treason.* It is a strikingly *brief* list by contemporary standards: in seventeenth-century England, there were roughly fifty capital crimes. In the eighteenth century there were more than one hundred.

Simplicity was also a goal of Puritan rhetoric. Preachers

---

*Puritans had to interpret the Hebrew Bible without benefit of the Talmud or the extensive Jewish tradition of commentary and scholarship. For better or worse, the Talmud virtually bans the death penalty, by adding requirements and restrictions that make it nearly impossible to impose.

were warned not to arouse a congregation with rhetorical tricks or emotional appeals. Plain logic and straightforward arguments were a preacher's only fitting tools.

The Puritan passion for simplicity plays an important though neglected role in American history. Many Puritan churches—especially in Boston, the intellectual headquarters of Puritanism—eventually abandoned Puritanism for Unitarianism. The transformation occurred mainly in the later eighteenth and early nineteenth centuries. Puritans were devout; Unitarians were cool and rationalist. When the bright blaze of Puritanism was replaced by the pale flicker of Unitarianism, a spiritual vacuum appeared on the American landscape. Eventually it was filled by Americanism itself. The American Religion was the true heir of Puritanism.

But how could Puritan warmth have trailed off into Unitarian cool? One important part of the answer has to do with the doctrinal simplicity of Unitarianism, which held God to be one, not one-in-three.

I've described the rise of American Puritanism and sketched its character. We need only glance briefly at its decline—and then move on to its important contributions.

By the late 1600s a sharp reduction in Puritan piety was evident all over America, especially in New England. As early as the 1640s preachers complained that young people lacked religious seriousness. In the early 1700s came a religious revival. In the revolutionary era Puritanism was important to proto-American culture—but the public agenda was monopolized by politics, statecraft, and war. The churches suffered. They suffered even more after the Revolution, during years that have been called a "religious depression" in America. In the late 1700s and early 1800s Puritanism disappeared as a live force.

America's decision points are my topic in this book. I focus in this chapter on the momentous period in which the first Puritan settlers arrived in the New World. There is no way to say exactly when this period ended, but a New England theological conference or synod in 1662 confirmed that it was over. It introduced the Half-Way Covenant, a scaling-back of earlier standards. The Half-Way Covenant specified that, even if they could not claim that divine grace had entered their lives, the grown children of church members could be "part members" of their parents' churches. They were not allowed to participate in communion or church voting, but their own children could be baptized.

Thus the New England Way fell back into compromise and confusion. A perfect church is not easily achieved. The higher your kite soars, the more likely it will get tangled in branches you never foresaw.

The Puritans and America's Character

Americanism consists of American Zionism and the Creed. But a *worldview* accompanies the American Religion too—a collection of attitudes that seem "typically American." Of course "typical" attitudes aren't *everyone's* attitudes. Yet recognizably American attitudes do exist: anti-Americans see them clearly enough. Americans gain nothing by ignoring them. The groundwork for these attitudes, for America's personality, was laid in seventeenth-century Puritan communities.

Long before the United States became the world's only su-

perpower, many Americans showed the world a Puritan intensity and a Puritan sense of mission. Europeans interpreted
those attitudes as naïve idealism, naïve religiosity, and a naïve
unwillingness to face global realities. The European picture of
innocent, idealistic, childlike America blundering into a china
shop stocked with fine old European pieces and smashing them
all to bits is, of course, partly true; nearly all caricatures are.
But America's traditional view of Europe—as cynical, supercil-
ious, pompous, and corrupt—is partly true as well.

Europeans down to the present insult Americans by calling
them "Puritan." Americans sometimes insult Europeans by
calling them "cavalier" (that is, too casual, cynical, indifferent). The opponents in the mid-seventeenth-century English
Civil War were called Roundheads (or Puritans) versus Cava-
liers. That Americans and Europeans still insult each other
in seventeenth-century terms should give us pause. You can't
understand Americanism or its enemies without understanding
Puritanism and *its* enemies.

American approaches to three topics have been especially
important and characteristic: the military, education, and business. Americans have typically neither lionized military officers (with the exception of national heroes) nor despised
common soldiers; when the need arose, war in America was traditionally every man's duty. Americans have typically believed
that education is important for every citizen. And they have
usually regarded free enterprise as a social good, and successful
businessmen as admirable.

All these attitudes were originally Puritan.

For the Puritans, bravery and the willingness and ability to
fight counted heavily. The "American personality" has inher-

ited the Puritan tendency to associate bravery and fighting ability with piety. These attitudes are closely associated with the worldview I have called democratic chivalry.

William Bradford wrote of the Pilgrims in early days, "It was not long before they saw the grim and grisly face of poverty coming upon them like an armed man, with whom they must buckle and encounter, and from whom they could not fly." Whom they *must encounter*: nothing could be more typically Pilgrim or Puritan (or American!).

If you visit Cape Cod today and travel up toward Provincetown where the Pilgrims first landed, you will find a place called First Encounter. Bradford explained that a Pilgrim scouting party was eating breakfast when one of their sentinels rushed in shouting, "Men, Indians! Indians!" Shortly afterward "their arrows came flying amongst them."

The Pilgrims hoped to be friends with the Indians—and soon afterward they were. But this "first encounter" was a surprise attack, and the Pilgrims beat it off. Then they chased the beaten foe some quarter-mile into the unknown woods, shouting and shooting—just to make absolutely clear that the English settlers "were not afraid of them or any way discouraged."

All over the Puritan colonies every male aged eighteen or over was expected to own a flintlock and practice with it regularly on the commons or village green *and* go to a regimental muster every year—*and* take his turn standing nightly "watch and ward" against Indian marauders and wild animals—*and* be ready to defend his home and village any day, any night.

For American Puritans, soldiering was accordingly a respectable, vitally important occupation. Of course it was also an amateur occupation.

Europe has traditionally looked *way* down on enlisted men; mere soldiers came near the absolute bottom of the social scale. And senior officers came near the top. But just as Puritans (and later Americans) refused to look down on soldiers, they refused to glorify officers. Americans were slow to fight but were able to fight ferociously; they laughed at militarism but respected the common soldier and expected every man to bear arms when the need arose.

★   ★   ★

Puritan attitudes toward education rank among this country's most valuable inheritances. Many churches in Puritan New England hired two ministers: one preacher, one teacher. Education was central to the church's mission. (Once again Puritan America showed its unwitting predilection for Jewish attitudes: a Jewish clergyman is a *rabbi*, meaning "teacher.")

Many sixteenth- and seventeenth-century Englishmen learned to read *using* the Bible specifically in order to *read* the Bible. The English Bible was a needle that punctured the ancient weave of medieval ignorance, pulling whole nations behind it; the Bible pulled the English-speaking masses into the modern world by teaching them to read. English Puritans often sponsored the publication of cheap editions of the Bible. Puritans in general famously refused to have "dumme dogges" for ministers (a reference to Isa. 56:10). Only an educated person could be a Puritan. ("No uneducated man can be truly pious," in the words of the Talmud.)

In the Puritan settlements of New England, parents were ordinarily required either to teach their children to read or to send them to school. Villages maintained primary schools, and some larger towns had tax-supported secondary "grammar schools." In his classic *Public Education in the United States* (1934), E. P. Cubberley wrote that the Puritans, "more than any others, gave direction to the future development of education in our American States."

Or as Cotton Mather wrote in 1710,

> If any children in the neighborhood are under no education don't allow 'em to continue so. Let care be taken that they may be better educated, and be taught to read, and be taught their catechism and the truths and ways of their only savior.

Puritans believed that God *wanted* an educated public.

★　★　★

Traditionally business, commerce, and hard work are more reputable in America than in Europe; and America, not surprisingly, has usually been a better place to *do* business. In Europe it used to be considered admirable to have nothing to do, to enjoy absolute leisure; in America such idleness has always been contemptible. Puritans worked hard. The Lord, they believed, expected it of them. They spoke of the "gospel of work"; the Lord approved of hard work and successful businesses, as far as they could tell. Non-Puritan Americans noted and often adopted these Puritan ideas. Shipowning merchants were at the top of the social hierarchy in the American colonies, along with clergymen and the small but growing professional class.

The American talent for business and the organization of economic activity emerged early. Remember, of course, that if Puritanism encouraged businessmen, it also *attracted* businessmen. Most Puritan colonies started life with populations that were well stocked with actual or aspiring businessmen and merchants.

During its first two planting seasons, however, Plymouth Plantation was a farming commune: everyone worked at food production and community chores; the results were doled out to each Pilgrim family according to need. It was pure socialism.

But the results were catastrophic. And so "at length," Bradford writes, the governor (namely himself) "gave way that they should set corn every man for his own particular," in other words for his own household, "and in that regard trust to themselves." Bradford "assigned to every family a parcel of land, according to the proportion of their number ... This had very much good success, for it made all hands very industrious." The result proved the falseness of the idea "that the taking away of property and bringing in community into a commonwealth would make them happy and flourishing."

This striking passage ought to appear on page one of every economics textbook on the planet. It gives the First Law of Business in a remarkably terse, persuasive way: do not force people to work for "the common good," or they will barely work at all. Allow them to work for themselves and their families, and they will work as hard as they have it in them to work. The Pilgrims found that out the hard way. Most Americans have believed it ever since.

The Biblical Roots of Americanism

Americanism came to consist of a Creed *in the context of* the doctrine of American Zionism. Puritanism played the decisive role in shaping American Zionism.

John Winthrop wrote in 1630 that the Lord was "jealous of our love and obedience, just as He told the people of Israel, 'You only have I known of all the families of the earth; therefore will I punish you for your transgressions' " (Amos 3:2). This highly significant verse is cited constantly in Jewish literature to explain the idea of a "chosen people." Quoting from memory, Winthrop omitted an important word; the verse actually reads "I will punish you for *all* your transgressions." Every single one. That is the price of being blessed or "chosen." (The King James Bible reads, "Therefore I will punish you for all your iniquities.")

The prophet Amos delivered this message from God to God's own chosen people. Today, Winthrop implies, Amos would have delivered it to *us*, the Puritans of the New World. *We* are the ones who are uniquely, intimately close to God. *We American Puritans are God's new chosen people.* Therefore, Winthrop concludes, we Puritan colonists will be held to the uniquely high standard that originated in God's relationship to Israel.

There are countless similar references in Puritan writings. The eminent theologian Thomas Shepard wrote:

> What shall we say of the singular providence of God bringing so many shiploads of His people through so many dangers, as upon eagles' wings, with so much safety from year to year?

He echoes two Hebrew verses. "Ye have seen what I did unto the Egyptians, and how I bare you on eagles' wings, and brought you unto myself" (Exod. 19:4). And "They that wait upon the Lord shall renew their strength; they shall mount up with wings as eagles; they shall run, and not be weary; and they shall walk, and not faint" (Isa. 40:31). Thus Shepard restates Winthrop's message: the Puritans of New England are ancient Israel reborn; they are God's new chosen people.

Shepard continues:

> . . . which gives us cause with Micah 7:18 to say: "Who is a God like our God, that pardoneth iniquities, and passeth by the transgressions of the remnant of His heritage; even because He delighteth in mercy?"

God promised that a *remnant* of Israel would survive. (Many Jews died during the Babylonian Exile, but a remnant survived and returned to Jerusalem to start building a new temple.) Shepard tells us that the New England Puritans are another sacred remnant, who can and must count on God's mercy.

And after all, the American Puritan experience really did suggest ancient Israel's. These God-obsessed men, women, and children had fled a "house of bondage," as it seemed to them, and after a dangerous voyage, "after long beating upon the Atlantick ocean," as Cotton Mather put it, they had reached pagan land, where they struggled to establish themselves. "The Lord hath brought us hither through the swelling seas," wrote Winthrop in 1643, "through perils of Pyrats, tempests, leakes, fyres, Rocks, sands, diseases, starvings." Bradford's story of the Pilgrims' terrible first winter is famous. Roughly half the hundred-odd settlers died that winter of hunger, disease, and exposure. At the worst times, "there were but six or seven sound persons" to nurse, feed, and care for the whole group. "Inexpressible the hardships to which this *chosen generation* was now exposed!" wrote Mather of the Pilgrims' first winter: among the new chosen people, these were *especially* chosen—and hardships are always the fate of the chosen. American Puritans believed that they deserved to compare themselves to ancient Israel.

The analogy to Israel recurs constantly. In fact, the American Puritan colonists felt kinship not only with the Israelite nation but with the Hebrew Patriarchs themselves—Abraham, Isaac, and Jacob, Israel's founding fathers. Mather compared "this remove of our fathers to that of Abraham." God's covenant with the Patriarchs marked the future nation as a blessed or chosen one. Israelites had special obligations to God, and vice versa. In return for God's blessing, His promise to make Israel a great nation and allow it to settle in the promised land, Israel was required to follow God's commandments—above all to be holy and "choose life."

Puritans likewise recognized a special obligation to choose life and be holy. They too believed themselves to be a chosen people. "We are entered into Covenant with [the Lord] for this work," John Winthrop wrote; "we shall find that the God of Israel is among us."*

---

*The Puritans were obsessed with the Hebrew Bible and their resemblances to ancient Israel. But they were not "crypto-Jews" or aspiring Jews. Most had no dealings with Jews. A few Puritans had studied Hebrew; some of them made friends with their Jewish tutors. Late in life William Bradford himself began studying Hebrew, so he might behold "the ancient oracles of God in their native beauty." But the American Puritan community as a whole never put itself out to befriend Jews, or to urge that Jews be tolerated or well treated. Ancient Israel enthralled the Puritans; Jews did not. On the other hand, Armand Laferrère writes that John Calvin's teachings "gave rise to the well-documented philo-Semitism of Cromwell Republicans, Scottish Presbyterians, and various non-conformist churches; later, they pervaded a large part of American Protestantism." See "The Huguenots, the Jews, and Me," *Azure*, Autumn 2006, p. 67.

So America's Puritans were the new chosen people. And naturally they regarded *America* as *the new promised land.*

Even before Winthrop and his group set out for Massachusetts, John Cotton (Mather's grandfather) preached them a sermon on this verse from II Samuel: "Moreover I will appoint a place for my people Israel, and I will plant them, that they may dwell in a place of their own, and move no more" (II Sam. 7:10). God had "planted" Israel in the promised land; He would plant these Puritans in a new promised land. The sermon likened Puritans en route to America to biblical Jews headed for Israel. The Puritans would inhabit their new settlements, Cotton said, "as well by gracious promise as by the common, and just, and bountiful providence of the Lord." *By gracious promise*—America, a *promised* land. (Cotton later joined his fellow Puritans in America and became a founder of the New England Way.)

During the voyage Winthrop himself composed an elaborate comparison between the Puritans and ancient Israel. Bradford reports that his people had no choice but to camp, on arrival, near their landing place on the Massachusetts coast. They had no reason to think they could do better elsewhere; they could not, "as it were, go up to the top of Pisgah to view from this wilderness a more goodly country." He saw no need to explain this reference to Moses gazing at *his* promised land from atop the Pisgah mountains before his death (Deut. 34:1).

Bradford makes another pregnant comparison between the Pilgrims and ancient Israel. Once the Pilgrims had landed in the New World, he writes, "What could now sustain them but the Spirit of God and His grace?" He continues,

May not and ought not the children of these fathers
rightly say: "Our fathers were Englishmen which came
over this great ocean, and were ready to perish in the
wilderness; but they cried unto the Lord, and He heard
their voice and looked on their adversity," etc.

He is paraphrasing Deuteronomy 26:5ff. Biblical Israelites were
commanded to speak these verses when they brought the year's
first fruits to the Temple and publicly recalled the Lord's gift
of the promised land. Bradford is again equating the arrival
of Englishmen in Plymouth, Massachusetts, with the arrival of
Jews in Israel.* (These same verses play a central role in the
Haggadah recited by Jews on Passover, although Bradford
wouldn't have known that—he singled them out on his own.)

These two ideas, that American Puritans were a *new chosen
people* in a *new promised land,* are the basis of American Zionism. There are countless reflections of these beliefs in American thought and literature.

Thomas Jefferson himself, favorite founder of the modern
secularists, relied on just these beliefs in his first inaugural address (as I'll discuss in chapter 4). American Zionism was a crucial part of Abraham Lincoln's worldview. And given today's
war in Iraq, we hear much about "Wilsonianism"—a foreign

---

*The historian Samuel Eliot Morison's scrupulous edition of Bradford's
journal is the scholarly standard, but it's not clear that Morison recognized
that these verses were a biblical paraphrase. Bradford himself left the point
implicit. But you can't really understand the Pilgrims *or* Puritans in general
unless you know the Hebrew Bible. Sadly, people who have this elementary
knowledge have rarely bothered to study the Puritans, and people who study
the Puritans have rarely bothered to know what the Puritans knew.

policy in which America undertakes to create a safer *and better* world. But why *better*? Why not stop at "safer"? Because of what you are, said British prime minister Tony Blair in an address to Congress; willingness to butt in on the side of right is what America is all about. But again, *why*? Because America has always considered herself "marked and chosen by the finger of God," a nation blessed by God far beyond what she deserves. And God expects something in return, namely *chivalry*: willingness to intervene on the side of right. To set forth "asking His blessing and His help, but knowing," as John Kennedy put it, "that here on earth God's work must truly be our own." And what is "the side of right"? What is "God's work"? The Creed answers, loud and clear: liberty, equality, and democracy. By spreading them, you do God's work.

American Zionism was important to the Puritan settlers themselves in more basic ways. Their sense of obligation and nearness to God helped keep them going in hard times, and it made their tiny settlements seem hugely important. Every American owes much to these brave and devoted settlers—who were sustained in turn by their American Zionist beliefs.

The Puritans felt most keenly the inspiring sense that the Lord had sent them on a sacred mission when it mattered most—at the very start. "It is not with us as with other men," one Pilgrim settler wrote home to England, "whom small things can discourage, or small discontentments cause to wish themselves home again." I have mentioned the Pilgrims' deadly grim first winter. When the *Mayflower* set sail again in April, returning to England at the end of that awful ordeal, not one settler returned along with her.

The Puritans' conviction that their promised land would be

a light unto the nations, a city on a hill, was in a sense borne out within their lifetimes. By midcentury the tiny Puritan settlements of the early 1600s were soundly established. Bradford, as I mentioned in chapter 2, wrote extraordinary words in his chronicle:

> Thus out of small beginnings greater things have been produced by His hand that made all things out of nothing, and gives being to all things that are; and as one small candle may light a thousand; so the light here kindled hath shown unto many, yea, in some sort, to our whole nation.

A powerful image, and a perfect one for America's self-conceived mission—to be a pillar of cloud by day and fire by night, to light the whole world to the promised land; to be the Statue of Liberty with raised torch lit, come to life.

In sum: passionate belief in the community's *closeness* to God and its obligation *to God and the whole world*—*Americans as a new chosen people, America as a new promised land*—that is American Zionism. And democratic chivalry, a powerful (though unnamed) force throughout American history, follows directly from American Zionism.

★ ★ ★

We hear from the Puritans not only American Zionism but premonitions of the Creed itself: liberty, equality, democracy.

These concepts don't emerge from the Bible and Christianity only; the Puritans were Englishmen, inheritors of a long tradition of English liberty and law. English *and* Judeo-Christian traditions were important to Puritan thinking. Yet nowadays we often neglect the fact that liberty, equality, and democracy all had biblical roots, as the Puritans understood them.

The desire to achieve liberty for the group, if not the individual, motivated Puritan settlement in the New World. Puritan settlers sought religious freedom but *also* social freedom to build society in a godly new way. In a quick note dashed off in 1647 a New England official named Samuel Symonds wrote that Puritanism "causeth the solid Christians to prize the rare and rich liberty and power which god hath given them, and they have deerly purchased." New England's Puritan settlements did not offer easy lives, but they did offer "rare and rich liberty." And eventually *religious freedom for our community* evolved in two ways: *religious freedom* became freedom in general; *for our community* became "for all mankind."

The Exodus story had a large effect on the creation of Americanism. The seminal influence of the Bible story is clear in a series of major American literary works: Samuel Mather's *Figures and Types of the Old Testament* (1673), Cotton Mather's *Magnalia Christi Americana* (1702), a history of seventeenth-century New England, and Jeremiah Romayne's *The American Israel* (1795).*

Puritan "freedoms" were limited and tentative. The Puritans believed in religious freedom—for themselves. If you were not a Christian of exactly the right kind, you had the freedom to keep your mouth shut or leave town. But Roger Williams was a Puritan too, and he founded Rhode Island as a Puritan community with religious freedom for all.

Outside the special case of Rhode Island, the limited freedoms of the Puritan community laid the basis for larger, roomier ones—

---

*See David Lyle Jeffrey, ed., *A Dictionary of Biblical Tradition in English Literature* (Grand Rapids, Mich.: William B. Eerdmans Publishing, 1992), q.v. "Exodus."

as the rough, raw homes, farms, and churches of 1630s Boston laid the basis for the more comfortable Boston of the revolutionary era. Tentative, preliminary settlements became thriving towns. Tentative, preliminary freedoms became thriving human rights.

Equality is the trickiest element of the Creed to trace. American Puritans ordinarily did *not* believe that *all men are created equal.* But we do find this doctrine foreshadowed by Alexander Whitaker, as religious freedom is foreshadowed by Roger Williams. Whitaker was an Anglican rather than a Puritan minister; in 1613 he sent to England for publication an essay called "Good Newes From Virginia." American Indians must be well treated by European settlers, Whitaker asserted; after all, "One God created us, they have reasonable soules and intellectuall faculties as well as wee; we all have Adam for our common parent: yea, by nature the condition of us both is all one."

In short, all men are created by God, and all have the same rational souls and the same common parent; thus *all men are equal*—"by nature the condition of us both is all one," "both" meaning Englishmen and Indians, Christians and pagans. So it *is* possible to read the Bible and find the equality of man at the very beginning.* But where did the founding fathers *actually*

---

*In fact the Jewish religious tradition drew this conclusion many centuries before the European settlement of America. A celebrated passage in rabbinic *midrash* asserts that the "greatest general principle in the Torah" is the verse that reads, "These are the generations of Adam" (Gen. 5:1), because it tells us that all men have the same parents, and thus all men are equal. In another *midrash* God asks Moses, "Do I care about distinctions among people? Whether it is an Israelite or Gentile, man or woman, male slave or female slave, whoever does a good deed shall find its reward." Another *midrash* notes that men treat the rich and poor differently, but "God does not act that way; all are equal before him, women, slaves, rich and poor."

find it when Thomas Jefferson wrote and the founders endorsed the Declaration of Independence? Abraham Lincoln had a fascinating theory, which I'll discuss later.

★ ★ ★

I have discussed liberty and equality. Last comes democracy.

Modern democracy had its tentative beginnings in the Puritan colonies. In July 1619 twenty-two "burgesses" met in a church in Jamestown, Virginia: democracy's debut in America. There were many restrictions, but it was a start.

Slightly over a year later the Mayflower Compact was signed, in November 1620, off Cape Cod. The Pilgrims were also sponsored by the Virginia Company, but they had landed way outside its jurisdiction. So they improvised a government of their own on the spot. The result was the famous Compact, by which the settlers agreed to be governed by majority decision until more permanent arrangements were made. It was another small but significant step.

I have mentioned the democratic arrangements in the early years of Massachusetts Bay. The first written constitution of modern democracy was inspired not by democratic Athens or republican Rome or Enlightenment philosophy or British commercial practice but by a Puritan preacher's interpretation of a verse in the Hebrew Bible. The Fundamental Orders of Connecticut are the "first written constitution of modern democracy." (The historian G. P. Gooch was the first to refer to them this way, in 1914.)

They were drawn up in response to a sermon of 1638 by Thomas Hooker before the general assembly in Hartford. Hooker based himself on a biblical verse in which Moses is addressing Israel in the wilderness: "Take ye wise men, and understanding, and known among your tribes, and I will make them rulers over you" (Deut. 1:13). By "take ye" Hooker understood, as other commentators have also, some sort of democratic choice. He interpreted the verse to mean that "the choice of public magistrate belongs unto the people, by God's own allowance . . . The foundation of authority is laid, firstly, in the free consent of the people."

Pastors continued to cite this verse, in connection with the powerful denunciation of monarchy in I Samuel, to mean that the Bible *required* democracy. Various sermons repeated this assertion up to and during the Revolution and in the years following.

In short, American Zionism was launched and the Creed was broadly hinted at by America's Puritan colonists. America's enemies call us "the Puritan nation"; for Americans that phrase should be a source of pride.

CHAPTER 4

REVOLUTION AND THE AMERICAN CREED

The Revolutionary War completed the preliminary shaping of Americanism by codifying the American Creed. Puritan colonists had premonitions of liberty, democracy, and even equality. But the revolutionary generation made these values explicit. Simultaneously it refined the doctrine of American Zionism.

Most Americans think of the American Revolution, the Declaration of Independence, and the Constitution as expressions of a rational, secular, Enlightenment spirit. But Christianity (especially Puritanism) and American Zionism were crucially important in shaping the drive for independence and the new American state. American Zionism made many colonists believe that they were oppressed by George III just as Israel had been oppressed by Pharaoh in Egypt. It made them believe also that they could count on God's help against huge odds, just as Israel had counted on God's help, and that their new nation should be a righteous democratic republic, just as ancient Israel was presumed to have been—before it rejected God's good advice.

These points of contact between American experience and biblical narrative were no casual curiosities. Imagine that your child had innocently retraced young Michelangelo's or Einstein's early life. You might expect big things of him. And if your own community had retraced the experience of God's chosen people—where could such a community be headed? No doubt toward an astonishing destiny. This sense of mission, of a magnificent destiny just over the next rise, haunted American thinking from the very first, and it still does.

The American Creed was no abstract doctrine invented by philosophers to entertain other philosophers. It was a distillation of biblical (especially Old Testament) principles as American Puritans understood them. It was a miniature Bible commentary, offering a supercompressed version of the Bible's ideas about man and the state. The American Creed combined with American Zionism yielded a full-blown American belief system. These beliefs would be refined further; they would eventually supersede Puritanism and become *the* American religion. In short, the revolutionary generation didn't merely create a new nation—it created a new force in the world's spiritual history.

I begin this chapter by discussing the familiar idea of an American Creed. Then I look briefly at the history of the revolutionary period. I conclude by examining the ways in which the partial, tentative Creed that emerged from the 1600s was transformed during the revolutionary era.

All these topics presuppose that religious faith played a big part in the American Revolution. Yet many thinkers—"secularists," for convenience—believe just the opposite: that the revolutionary generation approached life in a radically different spirit from the grim and scowling seventeenth century. Somehow a bunch of austere Puritans metamorphosed into affable

Enlightenment philosophers, debating the nuances of the social contract over their colonial cappuccinos.

And there does indeed seem to be a break in American intellectual history. The Declaration of Independence seems to reflect rationalist Enlightenment philosophy, not the passionate Puritanism of seventeenth-century New England. The Declaration appeals not to the Bible but to reason and nature and "nature's God." Governments, it says, are instituted among men to protect mankind's inalienable rights; when government becomes destructive of this end, the people have a right to create a new government. These don't sound like biblical ideas. The Bible never discusses inalienable (or any other kind of) rights. It never formulates conditions under which the people may abolish their government and create a new one. What inspired the Declaration, and what thinking lay behind it?

In 1962 the eminent historian Carl Bridenbaugh wrote,

> No understanding of the eighteenth century is possible if we unconsciously omit, or consciously jam out, the religious theme just because our own milieu is secular. The era of the Enlightenment was far more an Age of Faith (and Emotion) than an Age of Reason.

In other words, if the philosopher John Locke appealed to eighteenth-century Americans, that was because Locke's ideas harmonized with the Bible-inspired worldview of colonial thinkers. There's nothing startling in this idea; Locke himself turned repeatedly to the Bible as an authority. Jonathan Jacobs writes that "political theorists such as Grotius, Hobbes, Harrington, Locke, and others" were "united by the Hebraic tradition serving as their reference point." "For many seventeenth-century Protestant thinkers, the paradigm and origin of law, covenant, and nation was to be found in the Hebrew Bible."* Other scholars have made similar assertions.

I've spoken repeatedly of Puritans, but naturally there were many other Christians in the colonies. Episcopalianism or Anglicanism was often associated with British rule and opposition to independence.† Puritans and Anglicans may have disagreed on occasion, but on other occasions the various denominations got along. " 'Twas a special pleasure to me, on my first arrival in America among the friendly Philadelphians," one settler wrote regarding his arrival in 1770, "to observe how Papists, Episcopalians, Moravians, Lutherans, Calvinists, Methodists, and Quakers, could pass each other peaceably and in good temper on the Sabbath, after having broke up their respective assemblies." The rich complexity of religious life in the American colonies set them apart from Britain, and helped create a sense of what "America" meant.‡

In this religious hodgepodge the Bible and Christianity (broadly defined) were immensely important unifying influ-

---

*Jonathan Jacobs, "Return to the Sources: Political Hebraism and the Making of Modern Politics," *Hebraic Political Studies* (Spring 2006), 328, 334.

†The Anglican Church in America was the local branch of the Church of England, England's "established" or official church. After the Revolution the Anglican Church reconstituted itself as Episcopalian.

‡Carl Bridenbaugh writes, "The most 'American' fact about the English colonies, aside from the huge natural environment, was their varied religious composition and ecclesiastical organization, which figured far more in the lives of most of the inhabitants than government and politics."

ences. When George Washington spoke repeatedly to his troops
of their Christian duties, he knew that "Papists," Episcopalians,
Moravians, Lutherans, Calvinists, and Methodists would all understand.

An American Creed

"American Creed" is a phrase that seems to have been used first
by Gunnar Myrdal in his celebrated book *American Dilemma*
(1944). He defined the Creed as "the essential dignity of the individual human being," "the fundamental equality of all men,"
and "inalienable rights to freedom, justice and a fair opportunity." The United States was the first nation to be founded on
these principles. But the basic idea of the Creed goes back much
further than Myrdal.

Thomas Jefferson wrote a sort of Creed into the Declaration
of Independence. "Life, liberty and the pursuit of happiness" is
still the best-known version of America's Creed. But it doesn't
say much about distinctly *American* beliefs. Happiness per se is
not an American invention.

The inimitable Alexis de Tocqueville found that Americans
agreed on "liberty and equality, the liberty of the press, the right
of association, the jury and the responsibility of the agents of the
government." In 1898 James Bryce listed six distinctly American
beliefs; Samuel Huntington paraphrases them as follows: "the sacred rights of the individual, the people as the source of political
power, government limited by law and the people, a preference
for local over national government, majority rule, and 'the less
government the better.' " In modern times Daniel Bell gave a
pithier Creed: "individualism, achievement and equality of opportunity." Samuel Huntington's own version of the Creed has

seven elements: "liberty, equality, democracy, individualism, human rights, the rule of law and private property."

U.S. schools used to promote an American "common faith," to use John Dewey's term for American-style democracy and humanism. In 1951 a National Education Association commission listed "the values which made America great"—a Creed that ought to be taught, the Association believed, to all American children. It included "the supreme importance of the individual personality," "common consent," "brotherhood," and "the pursuit of happiness."

Most of these formulations amount to the same thing, more or less. For purposes of this book, I will define the American Creed as liberty, democracy, and equality for all mankind. The American Religion consists of this Creed in the context of American Zionism.

Most formulations of the American Religion leave out the idea that Americans are a new chosen people in a new promised land. But this idea is just as fundamental to Americanism as the Creed. And the Creed, for its part, is just as biblical in origin as American Zionism.

The Revolutionary Era

In June 1774 deteriorating relations between Britain and the colonies came to a head when Britain responded to the Boston Tea Party with the Boston Port Bill.

Bostonians dressed as Mohawk Indians had pitched 342 chests of tea into the harbor—342 splashes or muffled crunches into the dark water; 342 bobbing wooden boxes. (By dressing up as American Indians, the settlers were appearing as their nonchurchgoing, wild-living alter egos.) The chests were dumped overboard so that no one would be tempted to pay the new tea taxes that Parliament had imposed. The colonists argued that Parliament had no right to tax America, because Americans were not represented in the House of Commons. "Neither is the city of Manchester," Britons replied; many English cities were not represented in the undemocratic, crazy-quilt parliamentary system of that era. The British had decreed, also, that tea must be distributed by agents of the East India Company only—thus shutting out American distributors and middlemen. Company tea was boycotted throughout the colonies. Boston's tea party was merely the boldest, most attention-getting reaction to British high-handedness.

The Port Bill was collective punishment: Boston Harbor would be closed for business until the locals decided to treat British authority with respect. As far as the locals were concerned, that would be never. In the meantime Boston was threatened with economic collapse. General Thomas Gage was appointed governor of Massachusetts and was ordered to impose new punitive laws; the harbor remained closed.

The locals were not happy. British authority collapsed in Massachusetts—except in Boston, where General Gage was building forts and preparing for armed conflict. The lower house of the Massachusetts colonial legislature responded in kind, formally taking control of the rest of the colony and beginning its own preparations for war.

Americans throughout the colonies were outraged at British behavior. Every colony but Georgia sent delegates to the first Continental Congress, which met in the fall of 1774 in Philadelphia. The fifty-six members of the Congress demanded more autonomy, questioned Parliament's authority to legislate for the colonies, and sent an appeal over Parliament's head to the king and people of Great Britain. The colonists still felt like

Englishmen and expected fair treatment from their fellow Englishmen back in "Old England." To make sure England got the message, Congress organized a colonial boycott of British goods and arranged to meet again in May 1775.

Puritanism encouraged many eighteenth-century Americans to distrust British rule. After all, the king represented the established church—the traditional opponent of religious dissent and Puritanism.

And the English government had persecuted Puritans back in the motherland (although not during the several decades of Puritan rule during the seventeenth century, when the Puritans intermittently persecuted everybody else). Furthermore, the Hebrew Bible that Puritans held so dear tends to be strongly anti-monarchy. The translation and marginal notes in the Geneva Bible emphasized this bias. A note on Daniel 6:22, for example, reads: "He did disobey the King's wicked commandment [in order] to obey God." Obedience to God takes precedence over obedience to wicked royal commands. When the midwives in Exodus disobey Pharaoh's order to murder all newborn Jewish males, a note says that "their disobedience in this was lawful." Soon afterward comes another note: "When tyrants can not prevaile by deceit, they burst into open rage." If kings become tyrants, the people's duty is to disobey.

Puritanism rejected bishops and clerical hierarchies. Puritans in America worried that an Anglican bishop might be sent over from England to preside over American Anglicanism. In seventeenth-century Britain, Puritan doctrine had gone so far as to inspire a rebellion against the King of England, followed by his capture and eventual execution. Several of the king-killers had taken refuge in colonial New England. Puritanism had a strong tradition of dispensing unceremoniously with unacceptable monarchs.

All of which makes it unsurprising that the strongest support for American independence (before and during the war) came from the Puritan community—especially from Congregationalists, Presbyterians, and Baptists. The Quakers were another Puritan-inspired denomination, but they had turned pacifist and were not inclined to support a war for independence (or for any other purpose).

Whatever Puritanism taught, George III had no intention of humoring a bunch of primitive, disobedient settlers—and British public opinion largely supported him. George III had begun his reign in 1760 with the intention of strengthening the power of the crown. Parliament, which might have moderated his military response to the unrest in the colonies, was controlled from 1770 to 1782 by a faction called the "king's friends," under Lord North as prime minister.

On April 14, 1775, General Gage was ordered to march seven hundred soldiers from Boston to Concord to destroy a colonial weapons cache. The patriot militia—the celebrated "minutemen"—gathered to oppose Gage's forces. The Revolution began with the flash, crack, smoke, and smell of muskets: and with sweat, burns, shattered limbs, and pools of blood; and with shrieks of pain and whoops of victory. It was the Battle of Lexington and Concord, April 19, 1775. The minutemen could just as well have stayed home with their families, had a good breakfast, and gone to work. But their blood was up, their God was present, and they cared so much for liberty and the nascent American Religion that they trooped off to take a lead ball in the stomach, if necessary. No anesthetics, antiseptics, antibiotics, or even *nurses* existed; those men truly *cared* for the cause they defended. "By the rude bridge that arched the flood, / Their flag to

April's breeze unfurled, / Here once the embattled farmers stood, / And fired the shot heard round the world." Once upon a time every child in America knew Ralph Waldo Emerson's lines.

Fifteen months later the second Continental Congress convened. As the war continued, colonial public opinion had swung from petitioning for better treatment to demanding independence. Most colonists continued to think of themselves as Englishmen and to respect Britain as the military superpower she was. But as American soldiers fought and bled on the battlefield, independence came to seem like the only acceptable outcome. By January 1776 George Washington himself had endorsed independence for the colonies. This transformation of public opinion was to repeat itself in subsequent wars. As casualties mount, the American public naturally searches for larger, deeper meanings in the fighting.

Nonetheless, historians estimate that only half of all American colonists wanted independence during the greater part of the war. Radicals and hotheads usually carry the day. Another quarter wanted to stay English, and the last quarter was neutral. On the other hand, Britain's military advantage was turning out to be less overwhelming than many colonists had feared. England was far away, and the colonists were fighting on their home turf. In most battles they were able to field more soldiers than the British. And the Continental Army could fall back into the interior, gaining strength as it retreated, while the pursuing British traveled farther and farther from their supply bases and Atlantic ports.

Drawing on a population that averaged around a quarter-million able-bodied men in the thirteen colonies, the Continental Army never numbered more than around eight thousand active soldiers. Many historians treat this low figure as a stain on American honor. But for the average young man on a farm or in a town, the American Revolution was a mighty abstract war. The colonists' enemies, their leaders insisted, were the king and Parliament—who were thousands of miles away. The overwhelming majority of colonists had never laid eyes on them. And the army was fighting on behalf of *all* the colonies—perhaps of a new nation. But the new nation didn't exist, and no one knew what sort of nation it would be. Virtually every nation in the world was some kind of monarchy. Would an American monarchy be fundamentally different from the British variety? Given all these natural questions and doubts, eight thousand men was pretty good.

February 1778 was the turning point: France, then Spain, then finally Holland joined the war against Britain. Still, the patriots hardly faced an easy war even after that point: by 1780 Congress was unable to pay the army regular wages, Continental currency was worthless, and supplies had to be requisitioned. The British captured Savannah—a heavy blow to patriots in the South. But the intervention of the French, and Washington's brilliant grasp of the war's central reality—as long as the American army survived in the field, Britain could not be victorious—proved decisive.* On October 19, 1781, General Cornwallis surrendered at Yorktown. Britain still held New York and Savannah, but she had lost the war.

* * *

The American Revolution changed the world in three stages.

Instantly, the Declaration of Independence and (later) the Constitution were discussed all over Europe. The Revolution was fascinating and inspiring to European peoples and nations

---

*See, for example, Joseph J. Ellis, *Founding Brothers: The Revolutionary Generation* (New York: Alfred A. Knopf, 2000).

who felt persecuted or repressed. Americans who visited Europe caused a sensation; Benjamin Franklin was the toast of Paris. And many Europeans who had witnessed the fighting in America enjoyed great prestige on their return: the Marquis de Lafayette and two future marshals of Napoleon's army; Tom Paine; August von Gneisenau, the future rebuilder of the Prussian army; and Tadeusz Kosciusko, future hero of Poland.

In May 1783 Ezra Stiles recited some of the Revolution's accomplishments in a sermon preached before the governor and general assembly of Connecticut:

> The progress of society will be accelerated by centuries by this revolution. The Emperour of Germany is adopting, as fast as he can, American Ideas of toleration and religious liberty: And it will become the fashionable system of Europe very soon ... So spreading may be the spirit for the restoration and recovery of long lost national rights, that even the Cortes of Spain may re-exist and resume their ancient splendour, authority, and control of royalty. [In other words, Spain might replace absolute monarchy with something resembling the English parliamentary system.] Benevolence and religious lenity is increasing among all nations ... The Emperour of Germany, last year, published an imperial decree granting liberty for the free and unmolested exercise of the protestant religion within the Austrian territories and denominations. The Inquisition has been, in effect, this year suppressed in Spain, where the King, by an edict of 3d November, 1782, proclaimed liberty for inhabitants of all religions.

In the medium term other European peoples and colonies were inspired to rebel. The French Revolution (beginning in

May 1789) was inspired by America's. The French people demanded power and a constitution and refused to be dominated by
the aristocracy. Yet France's revolution was utterly different from
America's. French society was segmented into classes, which the
United States almost wholly lacked (and still does). Puritan New
England had set the tone by rejecting hereditary titles and rank,
although it thereby deprived itself of wealthy prospective settlers. But in France the lower classes' hatred of the aristocrats fu-
eled the murderous blaze of an out-of-control revolution.

And if America lacked something France had, she had other
things France lacked. One was traditional English respect for individual liberty and distrust of authority. Another was a society-wide
tradition of reading the Bible. English Puritanism placed the people much closer to the Bible than Catholicism did in France. And if
the Bible was a radical book, it insisted also on the dignity of all
men and the evil of naked violence. (All people must turn away
from "the violence that is in their hands," says the King of Nin-
eveh when he is won over to the Lord's message as preached by the
prophet Jonah.) "In England there are sixty different religions, and
only one sauce": for generations this pithy thought was attributed
to the Enlightenment *philosophe* Voltaire, master of pith; nowadays it is attributed to the Neapolitan republican revolutionary
Francesco Caracciolo (1752–99). In either case it is worth pondering. France is the place for good food, England for good men. (Not
invariably, but often.) England has traditionally taken morality, religion, and the spiritual side of life more seriously than many other
nations have. America inherited this obsession and deepened it.

Latin America won its freedom in the nineteenth century in
a series of revolutions partly inspired by America's. American
independence sparked a series of liberal revolutions in Europe
that culminated in the struggles of 1848.

But the most important consequence had to wait. The American Revolution shaped the nation that emerged (at last) to reshape the world in the twentieth century and the twenty-first.

The American Israel

Which was a bigger influence on the founding fathers, Enlightenment philosophy or Puritanism and the Bible? Modern American secularists claim that they are acting in accord with the founders' vision, and that the founding fathers were mostly secularists at heart (especially the most intellectually influential founders, and Thomas Jefferson above all). Their antisecularist opponents—historians and thinkers attuned to the religious element in American affairs—point out that this nation was created first and foremost as a haven of religious liberty by intensely pious Christian believers. Religion played a central role in selling the populace on independence and in suggesting to Americans what sort of state they ought to build. The antisecularists argue that the secularist reading of the Revolution is antithetical to everything this nation stands for—or *used to* and *ought to* stand for.

Research and writing in modern times have been strongly biased toward secularism. Bridenbaugh detected a strong secularist current in 1962; it goes without saying that the current has only gained momentum since then.* We need to correct for this bias when we consider the motives and ideas of eighteenth-century

---

*I noted in chapter 3 that it is not quite clear whether the eminent Samuel Eliot Morison noticed all of Bradford's biblical references in his 1970 edition of *Plymouth Plantation*; another modern thinker believes that Morison did not do full justice to George Washington's religiosity. See Richard Brookhiser, *Founding Father: Rediscovering George Washington* (New York: Free Press, 1996), p. 144. There are similar examples involving other eminent historians.

thinkers. We should bear in mind also that intellectuals tend to overrate other intellectuals' effect on the course of history.

Religion is nearly always a more important influence on events than philosophy, for several reasons. The Bible is a lot easier to read and understand than most philosophy books are. And religion and the Bible are far more likely than philosophy to address the emotional crises of everyday life. (For many centuries sad or discouraged people have turned to the Psalms—not to Plato or Kant or Locke.) Among other things, the Bible is, furthermore, a brilliantly drawn storybook, full of colorful characters and incidents. Philosophers seldom tell stories.

A cultural elite that dotes on philosophy can make philosophy influential even if most people never read any themselves. But it's not clear that American elites *did* dote on philosophy—even in the remarkable revolutionary generation. Clergymen were an important part of the American elite; they preferred the Bible. And have a look at the voluminous correspondence between John Adams and Thomas Jefferson.* In a series of letters covering half a century and filling more than six hundred pages, Locke comes up in exactly one letter. (This is a letter by Jefferson late in the series—1820—referring to Locke's opinion on the relationship between an infinite God and finite created beings. Jefferson writes that "these however are speculations and subtleties in which, for my own part, I have little indulged myself.") Jefferson might have had the great philosopher on his mind more than he said. But Locke was scarcely at the top of Jefferson's list of important subjects for discussion with a learned fellow founder.

---

*Lester Cappon, ed., *The Adams-Jefferson Letters* (1959; reprint Chapel Hill: University of North Carolina Press, 1987).

Elsewhere Jefferson wrote that "the God who gave us life gave us liberty at the same time." Antisecularists suspect that ideas like this one carried far more weight than philosophical doctrine in late-eighteenth-century America. Antisecularists suspect also that sermons did more to put Americans in the mood to rebel than all the works of Locke, Paine, and their fellow philosophers put together.* When Jefferson referred to his countrymen in his first inaugural address as "possessing a chosen country, with room enough for our descendants to the thousandth and thousandth generation," he endorsed in effect the American Zionist vision of a new chosen people in a new promised land—and used biblical language (the thousandth generation) to drive the message home.

A poem called "The Rising" by Thomas Buchanan Read (1822–72) deals with the role of clergymen in inspiring Americans to fight, as a later generation remembered it. "The Rising" tells the story of a Virginia pastor named John Muhlenberg who preached a fiery farewell sermon, then threw off his ministerial gown and appeared before his congregation in full military regalia—whereupon nearly every man present enlisted to serve under him with the patriots against the British.

The pastor rose; the prayer was strong;
The psalm was warrior David's song;
The text, a few short words of might,—
"The Lord of hosts shall arm the right!"

*For this view, see for example Conrad Cherry, ed., *God's New Israel: Religious Interpretations of American Destiny* (Englewood Cliffs, N.J.: Prentice-Hall, 1971).

The founding fathers varied in their religious attitudes, but their views of man rested on religious foundations. The Declaration of Independence proclaims that man's inalienable rights come from his "Creator." Rebellious Americans appealed to "the Supreme Judge of the world" and relied for protection on "Divine Providence." The signers held their honor "sacred." Most of the founding fathers were religious (although not necessarily orthodox); some were profoundly religious. Most believed in religious toleration, but nearly all seem to have thought of religion as essential to national well-being. As George Washington wrote at the start of his celebrated Farewell Address (1796),

> Of all the dispositions and habits which lead to political prosperity, Religion and morality are indispensable supports. In vain would that man claim the tribute of Patriotism, who should labour to subvert these great Pillars of human happiness, these firmest props of the duties of Men and citizens.

The Continental Congress asked a committee consisting of John Adams, Benjamin Franklin, and Thomas Jefferson to design a seal for the brand-new United States. (Franklin and Jefferson are often ranked among the most secular of the revolutionary elite.) Their proposed seal shows Israel crossing the Red Sea, lit by the divine pillar of fire, with the motto, "Rebellion to tyrants is obedience to God." (The seal was never adopted, but a copy of the recommendation survives in the papers of the Continental Congress.) Bradford's beckoning candle, Winthrop's shining city, the pillar of fire—and eventually the Statue of Liberty with raised torch; they are all versions of one underlying image.

Undoubtedly the clergymen based their worldview on the Bible first and on Enlightenment philosophy second (or nowhere). Of course, clergymen were affected by Enlightenment thinking, and in some cases they tried to make Christian doctrine more appealing to rationalists. But their first allegiance was clear. Books, pamphlets, and newspapers were all important, but in the late eighteenth century the sermon was the most important connecting link between the average American and the wide world of ideas. Sermons helped lay the basis for the Revolution and for the creation of the American Republic. In 1777, for example, toward the start of the war, Nicholas Street preached in East Haven, Connecticut*:

> The British tyrant is only acting over the same wicked and cruel part, that Pharaoh king of Egypt acted towards the children of Israel some 3000 years ago.

The title of Street's sermon was "The American States Acting Over the Part of the Children of Israel in the Wilderness and Thereby Impeding Their Entrance into Canaan's Rest."

In 1783, soon after the war was won, a Dr. Banfield preached about God:

> 'Twas He who raised a Joshua to lead the tribes of Israel in the field of battle; raised and formed a Washington to lead on the troops of his chosen States. 'Twas He who in Barak's

*Sermon texts are from John Wingate Thornton, *The Pulpit of the American Revolution* (Boston: Gould and Lincoln, 1860) and from Conrad Cherry, *God's New Israel: Religious Interpretations of American Destiny* (Englewood Cliffs, N.J.: Prentice-Hall, 1971).

day spread the spirit of war in every breast to shake off the
Canaanitish yoke, and inspired thy inhabitants, O America!

In that same year, Ezra Stiles delivered a sermon "upon the political welfare of God's American Israel."

Sermons like these make it clear that American Zionism remained central to American thought in the revolutionary generation. America, said Banfield, had triumphed like the ancient
Israelites over an evil enemy with God's help. Americans were
God's new chosen people. (After the war George Washington
was praised in biblical terms—compared most often to Moses,
Gideon, and Joshua—but sometimes also, to the deep embar-
rassment of preachers and theologians, to Jesus himself.)

Liberty

Liberty, democracy, and equality were defended by Enlightenment philosophers. But all three have biblical roots too. And
American colonists were well aware of those biblical roots.

In the founding generation's worldview, *liberty* (one element
of the solidifying American Creed) referred back to biblical
ideas about freedom and the Exodus. Liberty meant several
things: freedom from a tyrannical government that enslaved
the nation as a whole; freedom for each individual to speak his
mind and live as he pleased. Religious liberty is one important
aspect of the freedom to live as one pleases.

Liberty for the nation as a whole—freedom from tyrannical
government, from national enslavement—is the underlying
theme of the Exodus. It is also a theme of English history, and
American colonists considered themselves rightful inheritors of
English freedoms.

Religious liberty was especially important to America. Yet American Puritanism was distinctly *intolerant.* How did religious tolerance grow out of such intolerant beginnings?

The Puritan colonies held the roots of religious toleration, in two ways. First, although the Hebrew Bible does not by any means preach religious toleration, it does insist that aliens must be treated humanely, indeed with love. "The stranger that dwelleth with you shall be unto you as one born among you, and thou shalt love him as thyself; for ye were strangers in the land of Egypt" (Leviticus 19:34; there are other similar verses). From love of strangers to religious toleration is a logical step.

Furthermore (as I have already noted), Puritan New England included the colony of Rhode Island, where Roger Williams taught religious toleration to the world. Its royal charter stated that no resident may be in "any wise molested, punished, disquieted, or called in question, for any differences in opinion in matters of religion," so long as he "do not actually disturb the civil peace." Rhode Island too helped engender religious toleration in America.

It's also true, of course, that America in revolutionary times encompassed many denominations, nearly all of which had made some contribution to victory. On top of that, Enlightenment philosophy encouraged tolerance over intolerance.

In 1799, with the great republic safely established, Abiel Abbot delivered a Thanksgiving sermon "ratifying" American Zionism and its role in revolutionary thought:

> It has been often remarked that the people of the United States come nearer to a parallel with Ancient Israel, than any other nation upon the globe. Hence OUR AMERICAN IS-

RAEL is a term frequently used; and our common consent allows it apt and proper.

And Washington's early biographer Jared Sparks quotes a letter in which Washington said he was "sure there never was a people who had more reason to acknowledge a divine interposition in their affairs than those of the United States."

When he decided to retire, Washington spoke of wanting to sit "under his vine and under his fig tree"—in other words, to retire to Mount Vernon and the peace and quiet of country life. But the biblical phrase "under his vine and under his fig tree" is an iceberg, mostly submerged. The phrase occurs several times, and historians seem unsure about which passage Washington meant to quote. The best-known verses that speak of vines and fig trees are:

In the last days it shall come to pass, that the mountain of the house of the Lord shall be established in the top of the mountains, and it shall be exalted above the hills; and people shall flow unto it.

And many nations shall come, and say, Come, and let us go up to the mountain of the Lord, and to the house of the God of Jacob; and he will teach us of his ways, and we will walk in his paths; for the law shall go forth out of Zion, and the word of the Lord from Jerusalem.

And he shall judge among many people, and rebuke strong nations afar off; and they shall beat their swords into ploughshares, and their spears into pruninghooks; nation shall not lift up sword against nation, neither shall they learn war any more.

> But they shall sit every man under his vine and under
> his fig tree; and none shall make them afraid. (Mic. 4:1–4)

If Washington had these verses in mind, they were appropriate; he and his armies had indeed "rebuked strong nations afar off" and brought peace to the United States at last. By allowing the Bible to speak for him, Washington suggests that America has won a far-reaching peace ("they shall beat their swords into plough-shares, and their spears into pruninghooks") and would become a beacon for troubled peoples all over the world ("many nations shall come, and say, Come, and let us go up to the mountain of the Lord"). Implicitly he renews Winthrop's image of America as the shining city on the hill—the "mountain of the house of the Lord" that "shall be established in the top of the mountains."

Democracy

Nowadays many secular Americans associate religion with "theocracy" and suspect religious people of wanting to "impose their values" on everyone else. No doubt some religious believers are guilty as charged, but many are innocent. In any case, to associate Judeo-Christian faith with theocracy neglects the Bible's central role in the founders' view of democracy. Their model of democratic rule was neither Athens nor republican Rome; it was the sacred commonwealth of the ancient Hebrews.

In 1780, with the war under way, Pastor Simeon Howard of Boston was pondering the new nation's government. He reached the same conclusion Thomas Hooker had arrived at more than a century earlier, on the basis of the same biblical verses—plus a passage from the classical Israelite historian Josephus. Howard's conclusion was that America should be a democratic republic. His advice was as radical as it was straightforward, as avant-garde as it was Puritan, Bible-centered, godly. "In compliance with the advice of Jethro," preached Pastor Howard in May 1780,

> Moses chose able men, and made them rulers [over the Israelites in the desert]; but it is generally supposed that they were chosen *by the people.* This is asserted by Josephus, and plainly intimated by Moses in his recapitulary discourse, recorded in the first chapter of Deuteronomy. [italics added]

In 1788 Samuel Langdon (president of Harvard College) delivered a sermon in Concord, New Hampshire, whose title says it all: "The Republic of the Israelites an Example to the American States." The nineteenth-century historian William Lecky knew what many modern historians have forgotten: "Hebraic mortar cemented the foundations of American democracy."

Was ancient Israel (in the Bible's view) a democratic republic? The evidence isn't clear; scholars aren't sure. Certainly it was no "democratic republic" in the modern sense. But certain biblical passages condemn kings and kingship unequivocally. Many passages imply that the ideal national leader would be chosen by God but would not be a king. Political power seems to originate in the people's acclamation: "The men of Israel said to Gideon: rule over us, you and your son and your son's son, because you saved us from the hand of Midian" (Judg. 8:22). Gideon answers: "I will not rule over you, and my son will not rule over you; the Lord will rule over you!" (8:23) But Gideon does seem to rule, nonetheless.

It's interesting that the three circumstances that are part of the Bible's formula for political leadership—the leader is not a king, is chosen by the people *and* is chosen by the Lord—perfectly characterize the public's view of George Washington when he was elected president.

In any case, the important question is not what the Bible says about government; the important question is what conclusions Americans *drew* from the Bible. They noted the Bible's strong bias against monarchy. (America's powerful bias against monarchy was still a factor in world politics at the end of the First World War, when hints from America suggested that defeated Germany would be better treated by the United States if she transformed herself into a republic rather than a British-style constitutional monarchy.) Americans noted the role played by the people's approval. And they noted the central role played by the Lord—but had no way to incorporate divine approval into their new political system.

In an earlier sermon delivered in 1775 to the Congress of Massachusetts Bay Colony, Samuel Langdon had given a clear, comprehensive answer to the question: What conclusions should America draw from the Bible about government? (When he published the sermon, he used for his opening epigraph a verse from the Book of Proverbs: "As a roaring Lion and a ranging Bear, so is a wicked Ruler over the poor People.")

Here is Langdon's answer.

> The Jewish government, according to the original constitution which was divinely established, if considered merely in a civil view, was a perfect republic. The heads of their tribes and the elders of their cities were their counselors and judges. They called the people together in more general or particular assemblies,—took their opinions, gave advice, and managed the public affairs according to the

general voice . . . And let them who cry up the divine right of kings consider that the only form of government which had a proper claim to a divine establishment was so far from including the idea of a king, that it was a high crime for Israel to ask to be in this respect like other nations.

Given the biblical evidence that councilors and judges ruled in accordance with public opinion, Langdon assumes that they convened informal public meetings, listened directly to public opinion, and developed policy in a process of conversational give-and-take. The most powerful argument that could be marshaled against monarchy and in favor of democracy was the biblical argument: the Lord had condemned monarchy and endorsed government by the people (*and* the Lord).

Equality

And where does the idea that "all men are created equal" come from? From religion or philosophy?

As we have seen, in an essay dated 1613, "Good Newes From Virginia," Alexander Whitaker urged that American Indians be treated fairly. Whitaker knew that we were all created equal because the Bible tells us that Adam is our common father.

In the 1630s Whitaker's observation was echoed in the policy of Massachusetts Bay. The government banned liquor sale to Indians, on the grounds that Indians were more apt to get drunk than Englishmen. Then the government changed its mind. For it was "not fit," after all, "to deprive the Indians of any lawfull comfort which God aloweth to all men by the use of wine." A fascinating statement—which assumes that "all men" are equal before God, in some sense at least; and that it is therefore unjust to treat Christians one way and pagans another. No proof is offered. The equality of men before God is simply assumed, is self-evident.

So in writing the Declaration of Independence, Jefferson could have drawn on at least two types of argument in favor of equality. He could have drawn on philosophical arguments based on Locke, or religious arguments based on the Bible. Or both. He might also have drawn on English legal tradition.

Abraham Lincoln, for one, had no doubt about the real source of Jefferson's and his fellow founders' thinking. After quoting from the Declaration, Lincoln said:

> This was [the founding fathers'] lofty, and wise, and noble understanding of the justice of the Creator to His creatures. Yes, gentlemen, to *all* His creatures, to the whole great family of man. In their enlightened belief, nothing stamped with the Divine image and likeness was sent into the world to be trodden on, and degraded, and imbruted by its fellows. They grasped not only the whole race of man then living, but they reached forward and seized upon the farthest posterity.

In this extraordinary statement, Lincoln attributes the founding fathers' belief that "all men are created equal" to their "enlightened" awareness that all men of every race are "stamped with the Divine image."

Of course this is Lincoln talking, not Jefferson. Some thinkers believe that Lincoln was wrong about Jefferson and the founders. They argue that Jefferson was not a religious man, which is true. But it's easy to underestimate Jefferson's respect for biblical wisdom, which seems to have deepened as he got older.

Jefferson was no orthodox Christian. Arguably he was no

Christian at all, although he called himself one. He proclaimed himself a profound admirer of Jesus, whom he described as a human (not a divine) philosopher. He rejected Paul and Pauline Christianity. His religious beliefs were the "result of a life of inquiry and reflection," he wrote to his friend Benjamin Rush,

> and are very different from the Anti-Christian system attributed to me by those who know nothing of my opinions. To the corruptions of Christianity I am indeed opposed, but not to the genuine precepts of Jesus himself. I am a Christian, but I am a Christian in the only sense in which I believe Jesus wished anyone to be, sincerely attached to his doctrine in preference to all others, ascribing to him all human excellence, and believing that he never claimed any other.

Jefferson's public statements suggest also that biblical imagery moved and inspired him. George Washington had spoken of God in his inaugural addresses, setting a precedent. But Jefferson's language goes beyond the pro forma. His words *sound* biblical.

In his second inaugural, American Zionism emerges plainly. "I shall need," Jefferson said, "the favor of that Being in whose hands we are, who led our fathers, as Israel of old, from their native land and planted them in a country flowing with all the necessaries and comforts of life." So the analogy between America and ancient Israel becomes explicit. "Flowing with all the necessaries and comforts of life" is clearly an updated version of "flowing with milk and honey," the Bible's description of the promised land.*

The Declaration of Independence itself, with its seemingly

---

*In a circular letter of 1783 George Washington had described the New World as "abounding with all the necessaries and conveniences of life." By writing "flowing" instead of "abounding," Jefferson created a biblical reference.

evasive reference to "Nature's God," has been taken as a crypto-
secularist document. Jefferson's draft was fairly studied in its
avoidance of religious imagery. But Congress amended Jefferson's version to include two further references to God, as the
"Supreme Judge" and the source of "divine Providence."* And
to move from Jefferson to another of the most eminent among
the founding fathers, consider James Madison. Madison was the
main author of the Constitution and Bill of Rights. He was also
a principal defender of the Constitution during the ratification
period and coauthor of the Federalist Papers.

Madison approached human rights from an explicitly religious standpoint. Although he had always been a staunch, outspoken supporter of religious freedom and toleration, he was also
a serious student of theology—which he had studied at Princeton
(then the College of New Jersey) under John Witherspoon. (The
Scotland-born Witherspoon was president of the college and a
leading Presbyterian scholar.) After returning home to Virginia,
Madison continued his studies in theology and Hebrew. Many
years later, after he had been President of the United States and
had returned home once again, Madison summarized the effects
of a radical new doctrine that he had done much to propound and
defend. "The number, the industry, and the morality of the
Priesthood," he wrote in 1821—meaning the clergy in general—
"and the devotion of the people have been manifestly increased
by the total separation of the Church from the State."

Madison's thinking on the topic of human rights began with
"the inalienable duty of each rational creature to pay his Creator due adoration and thanksgiving." Nothing, he believed,

---

*See Michael Novak, *On Two Wings: Humble Faith and Common Sense at
the American Founding* (San Francisco: Encounter Books, 2002).

must be allowed to interfere with this supremely important duty. Hence man's first inalienable right was the right to praise God. Madison's view of rights resembles the colonists' view of liberty: a quest for religious liberty became a quest for liberty in a broader sense. For Madison, an inalienable right to praise God became a broader group of inalienable rights.

So what is the ultimate basis of "equality" in the American Creed? Locke and other Enlightenment philosophers did influence American thinking; so did the English legal tradition. But the Bible and the Judeo-Christian tradition did too. It's impossible to say which influence counted most. It is possible to *guess* that the Bible and religion were more important than anything else in forming the people's ideas, if not their leaders'.

And where does the idea of human rights itself come from? John Locke developed a "theory of rights," and the founding fathers are assumed to have got theirs from him. Certainly there is no "theory of rights" in Puritan teaching or, for that matter, in the Bible.

But a different biblical concept accomplishes basically the same thing. When man makes a covenant with God, he binds himself to obey God and strive for holiness—but *the Lord is bound also*. If man keeps faith, the Lord (under the Covenant) must support and sustain him. In other words, man acquires *rights* under the divine covenant. To accept the biblical idea of man's covenant with God is to acknowledge human duties to God, and human rights *derived from* God.

With these ideas, Americanism was born. But it was still unfinished. Americanism was incomplete until this nation's greatest prophet, preacher, and religious leader had accomplished his life's work.

CHAPTER 5

ABRAHAM LINCOLN, AMERICA'S LAST AND GREATEST FOUNDING FATHER

A braham Lincoln completed the work of the founding fathers and thereby became, in effect, the last and greatest of them. Lincoln and the Civil War completed the American Religion. It was Alexander Stephens, vice president of the Confederacy, who said that "with Lincoln the Union rose to the sublimity of religious mysticism."

Lincoln shows us a remarkable process, the transformation of one religion into another; Lincoln completed the transformation of Puritanism into Americanism. When it was complete, Americanism *was* Puritanism, in a new form. The American Religion had been assembling its forces gradually; Lincoln brought them alive. Although he believed deeply in God and the Bible and often spoke publicly about both, he was unsure of Christianity and had difficulty even calling himself a Christian. ("Mr. Bateman," he said once, "I am not a Christian,—God knows I would be one.") But he had no trouble talking about Americanism. Lincoln seemed to transfer his allegiance over his lifetime—we can practically see it happening—from Puritan Christianity to the biblical religion of Americanism.

To grasp the character of Lincoln's transformation, consider the Second Inaugural Address. Lincoln says that we have sinned against the Lord; the Lord has punished us; but (quoting the Psalms) "the judgments of the Lord are true and righteous altogether." And now, he concludes, we must resolve to *walk with* the Lord ("with firmness in the right as God gives us to see the right, let us strive on to finish the work we are in")—and sin no more.

There is nothing "political" or pro forma about the religious content of this speech; its topic is God, America, and the Civil War. Lincoln was president, but his text implied *I am speaking to you as a preacher does.* His audience was American citizens, but his speech implied *I will address you as congregants of a new church.* These "congregants" were a mixed multitude who followed many separate religions, but his speech implied *there is one religion you all share*—namely Americanism. When you speak of Americanism, the church is the nation; the congregation is every citizen. But the Lord and the Bible are the same as always. Lincoln takes the central ideas of Judeo-Christianity—sanctity and sin and faith, divine commandments and favor and punishment, mercy and charity and forgiveness—lifts each symbolically before the world, and consecrates each one to the new faith. This speech is the incandescent core of the American Religion.

Remember that Lincoln's words would have resonated in the minds of an audience that knew the Bible; whose minds were full of the Bible. When he closed by saying, "With malice towards none; with charity for all; with firmness in the right, as God gives us to see the right," some of his audience would have heard in their own minds another three-part formula: "What does the Lord require of you but to do justice, love mercy, and walk humbly with your God?"

This is a good place to remember Lincoln's recurring dream of a phantom ship making rapidly for some dark, mysterious shore. He associated that dream with Union victories, which seemed to follow in its wake. The dream was about a voyage nearing completion, a passage to an unknown place. No doubt he had many reasons to dream this way. But one reason might well have been the voyage of transformation by which Puritanism was converted to something new and mysterious ("with Lincoln the Union rose to the sublimity of religious mysticism"). The battle of Lincoln's life was to preserve America, for the sake of Americanism: for the sake of "conceived in liberty," "all men are created equal," and "government of the people, by the people, for the people."

Lincoln fought to preserve the Union; he ran the Civil War and won. But what did he do for America *spiritually*?

Lincoln transformed Americanism into a full-fledged, mature religion—not by causing America to embody its noble ideals but by teaching the nation that it *ought* to embody them. He changed Americanism by interpreting those ideals—liberty, equality, and democracy—not as words on parchment but as marching orders. By leading the fight to preserve the Union and free the slaves, he moved American reality a giant step closer to American ideals. "Washington taught the world to know us, Lincoln taught us to know ourselves," wrote Donn Piatt in a remarkably perceptive essay published in 1888.* (Piatt was a Union officer and military judge in the Civil War.)

*My quotations of Piatt are from Donn Piatt, untitled reminiscence in *Reminiscences of Abraham Lincoln by Distinguished Men of His Time* (New York: North American Review, 1888), pp. 477–500.

In the Gettysburg Address and the Second Inaugural, Lincoln produced the two greatest sacred narratives in the English language (outside of the English Bible itself); each is a guide to the Civil War and its meaning and to America's Religion, history, and experience as Lincoln understood them. The Gettysburg Address is the best statement we have of the American Creed. In the Second Inaugural, Lincoln delivered a Puritan message in the language of Americanism. The speech marked the transformation of Puritanism into the new American Religion.

To understand this achievement, we need to begin at the end of the revolutionary period.*

Everyday American History Begins

George Washington served two terms as president, from 1789 through 1797. When John Adams became president in 1797, the revolutionary period came to an end and ordinary, everyday American history began.

By the end of Washington's presidency, American Zionism and the American Creed existed in roughly their modern forms. But Americanism was immature, and an ugly, ominous fault line ran down its center: one day there would be an earthquake. The founding fathers understood that slavery and Americanism couldn't possibly coexist over the long term. The nation and the world understood that slavery invalidated the Declaration's message. "With the curse of slavery in America there was no

---

*In this chapter I rely, naturally, on many primary and secondary sources. Of the countless indispensable Lincoln studies, one is *most* indispensable for my purposes: William J. Wolf, *The Religion of Abraham Lincoln* (New York: Seabury Press, 1963).

hope for republican institutions in other countries," George Boutwell, treasury secretary in the Grant administration, wrote in retrospect. "In the presence of slavery the Declaration of Independence had lost its power: practically, it had become a lie. In the presence of slavery we were to the rest of mankind and to ourselves a nation of hypocrites."*

A nation of hypocrites. Many Americans knew and felt it. Lincoln changed it.

The first half of the nineteenth century was a difficult time for Americanism. When President Jefferson bought the Louisiana Territory from Napoleon in 1803, he secured U.S. navigation on the Mississippi and doubled the nation's size. But as Americans pushed eagerly westward—northerners establishing new free territories and states along the way, southerners new slave territories and states—"Manifest Destiny" became increasingly prominent in American thinking.

Manifest Destiny held that America's fate was to spread Christian, democratic civilization over the whole continent like a great breaker driving in from the Atlantic. It was the nation's destiny because Americans had passed a crucial test: they had created a new thing in modern history, a democratic, self-governing nation, in harmony with natural law and the Bible. So they had a "natural right" to expand. The New York journalist John O'Sullivan wrote in 1845 of "the right of our manifest destiny to overspread and to possess the whole of the continent which Providence has given for the development of the great experiment of liberty and federative self-government entrusted to us." Some unsubtle thinkers made

---

*George S. Boutwell, untitled reminiscence in *Reminiscences of Abraham Lincoln by Distinguished Men of His Time* (New York: North American Review, 1888), p. 134.

American expansion sound like a force of nature, pure and simple. If the Almighty didn't like it, His options were limited. It was just *obvious* that the whole great territory from the East Coast to the Pacific belonged to the United States of America.

But something that is obvious or "manifest" doesn't need biblical support; nor does it depend on American Zionism and its teachings about a chosen people in a promised land, and its duty to all mankind. If your destiny is manifest, anyone can see it. American Zionism has to do with the awe Americans felt in encountering a vast continent that was beautiful, richly endowed, and sparsely settled—"a chosen country," Jefferson said, "with room enough for our descendants to the thousandth and thousandth generation"; Americans were overwhelmed. Their thoughts are expressed most clearly in art, for example in paintings by the English immigrant Thomas Cole, who founded the Hudson River School. *View from Mount Holyoke* (1863) is a gigantic scene with a wild tangled hilltop, thunderclouds, and (far below) a sunlit valley where a golden-white river wanders casually through serene pastureland. In John Frederick Kensett's masterpiece *Lake George* (1869) the nuanced gray silver of the lake meets a subtle silver hill and a pale pewter sky. The landscape is a majestic living organism, gently dreaming.

Americans knew that God had blessed them far beyond what they deserved. But Manifest Destiny turned awe to smugness. It replaced feelings of wonder with those of entitlement. It was a nineteenth-century premonition of the welfare state, in which everything is coming to you and nothing is expected *from* you, and your duties are nil—except to collect what you're owed.

While Manifest Destiny emerged, Puritanism declined, losing its grip on American minds. Americanism itself, still plastic in its newness, sounded less like a heavenly choir and more like a brass band every day. Already it was deteriorating as a religious faith, as a way of interpreting the Bible that imposed strict responsibilities on Americans. It was deteriorating into an irreligious patriotism that struck serious people as blaring, blatant chauvinism.

The Civil War, as Lincoln came to understand it, changed all that. It restored Americanism to its original spiritual purity and readied it to take the place of dying Puritanism. And it pushed the United States toward compliance for the very first time with its own Creed.

In simplest terms, the American Religion sprouted on the spare, bare branch of Puritan Christianity. And the blossoms hid the branch. And the branch disappeared. Today *anyone of any faith* can celebrate those beautiful blossoms whether or not he believes in Puritanism or any other Judeo-Christian religion. Anyone can believe in and practice Americanism. (Yet America remains *the biblical republic*; that is her history and identity and will never change.)

In this chapter I will glance at the history of Lincoln and the war, then at the teachings of our last and greatest founding father.

Lincoln and the Civil War

What kind of name is Abraham? A strange one. It was not quite as strange in 1809, when Lincoln was born, as it is today—but it was strange enough. An informal survey of male first names in the Lincoln Memorial Album dedicated to his memory in 1883 suggests that William, John, George, James, and Charles were the leading five. There were more biblical names in evidence than you would find today—but not a single Abraham, except for the man to whom the book is dedicated (who also had a cousin named Abraham).

Lincoln's first name seems to have mattered to people. When he was president, people called him "Father Abraham." Troops on their way to Washington chanted, "We are coming, Father Abraham"—referring indirectly to the biblical patriarch, father of the Jews, who had meant so much to the Puritans.

Not only was the name strange, it was strangely apt. Young Abraham Lincoln doted on the Bible and on the Puritan masterpiece *Pilgrim's Progress* (also on *Aesop's Fables*). "He could repeat from memory many whole chapters of the Bible," according to the journalist and Lincoln's friend Noah Brooks,* who had another unusual biblical name—although not nearly so unusual as Abraham. Biblical language permeates Lincoln's extraordinary English. No other president knew the Bible as deeply and thoroughly.

As president, Lincoln was often compared to biblical heroes. The most moving comparisons came after his death. He was murdered six days after the Civil War's end. Naturally he was compared to Moses, who had led his people to freedom and died with the promised land in view but just barely beyond reach. Lincoln saw Americanism itself as a goal to struggle toward with all your might, *knowing* that you might never make it, knowing that it might seem farther and farther beyond your grasp as you learned more and more about God. "It is said in one of the admonitions of the Lord," Lincoln remarked, that

"As your Father in Heaven is perfect, be ye also perfect." The Savior, I suppose, did not expect that any human crea-

*My quotations of Brooks are from Noah Brooks, *Men of Achievement, Statesmen* (New York: Charles Scribner's Sons, 1894), pp. 175–222, and Noah Brooks, *Washington in Lincoln's Time* (New York: The Century Co., 1895).

ture could be perfect as the Father in Heaven; but He said, "As your Father in Heaven is perfect, be ye also perfect." He set that up as a standard . . . So I say in relation to the principle that all men are created equal, let it be reached as nearly as we can.

But the most important expression of Lincoln's belief that you must struggle toward truth and holiness even if you never arrive occurs in a phrase he applied to the American people. He called them God's "almost chosen people." If they had not made the grade yet, nonetheless they must keep on trying.

Lincoln has this strange distinction among many others: almost certainly he is the greatest man who has ever been photographed. When you look at his face, you see no ordinary man. In its gaunt strength, weary far-awayness, and sublime kindliness, it is a biblical hero's face. Lincoln was deeply attached to the Bible and in a curious way strengthens our faith in Scripture. His face in the old photographs makes biblical reality easier to grasp—as if we were looking at Isaiah, who lived so near to God that the heat seared him and he could barely stand it.

★   ★   ★

Lincoln was born in Kentucky and grew up in Kentucky, Indiana, and Illinois—on the western frontier, the ragged edge of a new nation. He was a child during the hard times that followed the War of 1812. The nation was poor. The West was dirt poor.

Brooks reported details about the frontier of Lincoln's childhood: "Thorns were used for pins, and bits of bone or slices of corn-cob were used for buttons"; "crusts of rye bread served as a substitute for coffee, and the dried leaves of currant bushes were used in place of imported tea." "Every man and boy was a hunter and trapper." Only when Lincoln's father remarried in 1819, after the boy's own mother died, did the family acquire such fancy articles as bedding, knives, and forks. Lincoln loved his mother, Nancy Hanks Lincoln, who died in 1818 when he was nine; he loved his stepmother Sally Johnston too. She was a widow with three of her own children. She became Abraham's loving mother also. Two different loving mothers is more than the usual share. It isn't guaranteed to turn you into a self-confident genius, but it couldn't hurt.

Lincoln's inborn abilities together with a frontier youth spent hunting and trapping, chopping and hammering, made him strong. "Physically, he was a very powerful man," wrote the painter F. B. Carpenter, who came to know him well. "His mind was like his body, and worked slowly but strongly."* Although he was a first-rate fighter, he was known among friends and neighbors as a peacemaker. "Lincoln's long arms invariably brought peace," wrote Noah Brooks. Lincoln was a walking embodiment of "peace through strength." (Embodied metaphors—metaphors expressed not in language but in reality—are more important than we give them credit for.)

As a child and teenager, he helped his parents manage their hard frontier life. But he had no intention of becoming a farmer like his father. As a young man, he worked as a laborer, steamboat pilot, and clerk in a country store. Clerk was the job he liked best; it left him plenty of time to read. In 1830, when the family moved to Illinois, he was twenty-one and stood six foot four. He first saw slavery in New Orleans, while working on a Mississippi flatboat. We are told that he hated it from the start.

*My quotations of Carpenter are from F. B. Carpenter, *Six Months at the White House* (New York: Hurd and Houghton, 1866).

Of course we don't often read about northerners encountering slavery for the first time and falling in love with it. But slavery did seem to make a big, bad first impression on many young northerners.

In April 1832 Lincoln had his only quasi-military experience. During a short fight with Indians in northern Illinois called the Black Hawk War, he joined the army and was elected captain of his company—and was discharged without having seen action.

He decided to become a lawyer. He read some books and picked up experience handling legal chores for friends and neighbors, and in March 1837 the Illinois Supreme Court admitted him to the bar. Meanwhile he was serving four terms as a Whig in the Illinois State Legislature, from 1834 to 1840; then he set up a law office in Springfield. In 1840 he was engaged to Mary Todd, who came from a good family and was part of the local aristocracy; but she was not, in the end, a brilliant acquisition. Five years earlier it seems he had fallen in love with Ann Rutledge, and they may have been engaged, but she died at age nineteen. In November 1842 Abraham and Mary got married. The next year their first son was born.

Many people noticed his sadness over the years and attributed it to deep pondering—which must be correct, at least partly. No man could ponder any deeper. But remember also that Lincoln's mother *and* stepmother had shown him the world-transforming power of mutual love with a woman. Life *with* such a woman (as wife or mother, sister, or daughter) is very different from life without one. Mary tried hard, and no doubt made him a better wife than many biographies concede. She was deeply devoted to him. But she proved incapable of measuring up to Lincoln's mother or stepmother. Pondering the contrast could not have made him happy.

She bore him four boys. Only the oldest, Robert, lived to adulthood. He and his father were never close. Lincoln loved the others gigantically, but Edward and William died during his lifetime—Edward at three, William at eleven. Lincoln stood by Mary, whose behavior during their life together grew increasingly bizarre. But it's hard not to suspect that his choice of a wife was a terrible mistake that made him sad and that that sadness was with him always. No doubt his devotion to the Union and his devotion to his personal union with Mary are somehow related. Either might grow uncomfortable; both were forever.

In August 1846 he was elected to Congress. His one term over, he returned from Washington to Springfield and plunged into lawyering—and more politics. He worked hard, did well, and made a name as one of the best lawyers in Illinois—celebrated for wit, fairness, and perfect honesty—and for winning cases. He made a good living at it.

Meanwhile the Civil War was creeping slowly over the horizon and subtly changing the quality of the light over the fields and towns of the new republic.

While Lincoln was growing up, northerners and southerners were pushing steadily westward. The Missouri Compromise of 1820 decreed that new states would be admitted to the Union in pairs, one free and one slave state together—a thought-provoking buddy system, good and evil holding hands. (The cotton gin, a 1793 invention for pulling seeds out of cotton, caused a huge expansion in the slave-based plantation economy of the South by making it profitable to grow cotton varieties that had never before been worth the trouble.)

In 1846, when the Missouri Compromise was roughly a generation old, the United States acquired vast new lands in the Mexican War. California was the first new state to be organized in former Mexican territory—and California was admitted to the Union as an unaccompanied free state, with no slave state as a partner. So the Missouri Compromise was done for, and a new arrangement was necessary. According to the Compromise of 1850, the North would enforce runaway slave laws to the South's satisfaction. Northerners hated to do it, and abolitionist sentiment grew. Abolitionists wanted slavery abolished with no compensation to slaveholders—and they denounced the Union itself as a slave-promoting institution. In 1852 *Uncle Tom's Cabin* appeared. Harriet Beecher Stowe's novel made slavery vivid and real and unsupportable to readers all over the North.

Two years after *Uncle Tom* the Republican Party was founded by northern Democrats and Whigs (as the Whig Party slowly disintegrated). Lincoln, who had become a prominent, respected personage, was one of the new party's founders. Its basic principle was *no further territorial expansion of slavery*.

The Illinois branch of the brand-new Republican Party opened for business in May 1856 at a Bloomington convention. Lincoln was asked for his advice. "Let us in building our new party," he said, "make our corner-stone the Declaration of Independence. Let us build on this rock, and the gates of hell shall not prevail against us." ("And I say also unto thee, That thou art Peter, and upon this rock I will build my church; and the gates of hell shall not prevail against it" [Matt. 16:18]. Lincoln had the Bible on his mind. And when he spoke in biblical terms, he could be sure his words would resound in the Bible-loaded minds of his listeners.)

For Lincoln, the Declaration was a rock for building on. Jesus foresaw a church built on the rock of Peter; Lincoln saw the Republican Party as a new kind of church. This is a key to the rest of his life.

In 1856 the Republicans nominated John C. Frémont for president. Lincoln campaigned hard in Illinois; he gave more than fifty speeches for Frémont. But Frémont lost. Two years later came the first big event of Lincoln's political life.

The Lincoln-Douglas debates of 1858 are the most famous in American history. The two men were fighting for an Illinois Senate seat. The Democrat Stephen Douglas held the seat; Lincoln wanted it. When the Republicans nominated Lincoln, his acceptance speech had included some controversial pronouncements: he had alleged, once again in the Bible's words, that *a house divided against itself cannot stand;* that the Union could not permanently endure half slave and half free. Again his words would have resonated among Americans with the Bible on their minds: "And if a house be divided against itself, that house cannot stand" (Mark 3:25). Lincoln proposed a series of debates with Douglas for the usual reason: he was the challenger and aspired to stand toe-to-toe with the better-known incumbent.

The Illinois state legislature chose Douglas anyway. (Many years would pass before the direct election of U.S. senators became law in 1913.) But Lincoln's first-class performance in the debates was noted all over the country, and he became a national figure.

In October 1859 John Brown led fellow abolitionists in a famous attack on the federal arsenal at Harpers Ferry, Virginia. Brown was a deep-dyed Puritan who wanted to free slaves and make trouble for the federal government. He said he was following the Lord's instructions. In a biblical republic there was nothing terribly unusual about such an assertion. But he was hanged anyway, in December. Henry Wadsworth Longfellow, the nation's best-loved poet, cited the Bible in response: "This is sowing the wind to reap the whirlwind, which will come soon."

("For they have sown the wind, and they shall reap the whirlwind: it hath no stalk: the bud shall yield no meal: if so be it yield, the strangers shall swallow it up" [Hosea 8:7].)

★　★　★

By 1860 the United States was a big nation. Its population of 31 million made it larger than Great Britain and nearly as big as France.

It was also on the verge of ruin. It was turning into two separate countries, identical in some ways but dead opposite in others—"countertypes" poised to hate each other. The North was a growing industrial giant, a junior version of Great Britain—but unlike Britain, it had a constant influx of immigrants to build its strength and a western frontier to draw off its more rambunctious citizens.

Northerners wanted protection from British industry; they wanted high tariffs to jack up the price of British manufactured goods. Americans would "buy American" or else pay through the nose. The North depended on free labor, of course; along with the rest of the civilized world, northerners found slavery increasingly disgusting.

Meanwhile the South was becoming Great Britain's handy little helper, like a colony only better: the British could enjoy all the fruits of slavery without dirtying their own reputation or shouldering any part of the moral burden. The British textile industry ingested huge helpings of southern cotton—produced by slave labor.

By 1860 anyone could see that slavery, like a once-raging forest fire, was dying at last all over the world. Civilized people could no longer stomach it. Slavery was abolished in the British colonies in 1833 and in the French colonies in 1848. The independent nations of Latin America abolished slavery during the first half of the 1800s.

Serfdom was a form of slavery; it forced landless peasants to live and labor where their masters ordered them to. It disappeared from western Europe at the end of the Middle Ages, but survived in Russia and in some parts of eastern Europe. In 1848 it was finally abolished in eastern Europe and in 1861 in Russia.

In the United States animosity between northern and southern states was reaching frightening intensity. North and South were like a man and wife who hate each other; but Lincoln (and many others) revered the institution of marriage and felt the same way only more so about the institution of the United States. People had died to create this Union. There was no such thing as divorce (or secession) in the Constitution. And even more important (Lincoln would have thought, with inexpressible, shattering sadness), it had all been so beautiful, once. This was George Washington's, Ben Franklin's, Thomas Jefferson's creation. Lincoln revered the United States profoundly his whole life.

Yet North and South acted like two different countries, like married people who live separately and barely talk. They had different economies, worldviews, and vital statistics. When America became independent in the eighteenth century, North and South had been roughly equal in population; by 1860 the North was way ahead.

As the contested divorce approached, western expansion was the flashpoint. The same ambitious energy that had pushed northerners westward drove southerners too, but the South had an added factor: slave populations increased as new generations were born. Southerners wanted to squeeze maximum profit out of slavery by creating new plantations out west. Northerners hated the idea of *new* slave states. Slavery itself was hateful; and besides, a new slave state was a state with no room for free labor.

Men working for wages couldn't possibly compete with captives working for free. This point was vital to northerners, and to Lincoln. Slavery and free labor could not coexist; or as Lincoln had put it in the biblical language that came so naturally to him and his listeners, a house divided against itself could not stand.

Early in 1860 Lincoln gave a speech at the Cooper Union College in Manhattan, in one of America's largest halls. Slavery must not, he proclaimed, be extended into new territories. And he closed by saying, "Let us have faith that right makes might, and in that faith let us, to the end, dare to do our duty as we understand it."

The Cooper Union speech was a great success. It was clear, Lincoln's White House secretary John Nicolay wrote later, that Lincoln had "taken New York by storm." Now he was no mere national figure—he was a fashionable one also.

The Democratic National Convention met in Charleston that year. Bitter disputes over slavery split the party and broke up the convention. The northern Democrats reconvened in Baltimore and nominated Lincoln's debating opponent, Stephen Douglas. The southerners met at Richmond, then reconvened in Baltimore. (Maryland was a slave state.) They nominated John Breckinridge of Kentucky.

North and South were now hurtling toward each other like steam locomotives head to head. Nothing could avert the crackup. But the Republican Party and its candidate tried.

The Republicans decided to move to the center for broader electoral appeal. So they chose Abraham Lincoln as their presidential candidate. Lincoln hated slavery but did not hate the South; he was a moderate.

The radical wing of the Republican Party was abolitionist.

Lincoln was no radical, and many abolitionists disliked and distrusted him.

He won the 1860 election with only 40 percent of the popular vote. The two warring Democrats split the rest. But even if the Democratic Party had not chosen this moment to saw itself in half, Lincoln would have won the electoral vote.

He showed what he was made of when he named his cabinet. While he was considering Salmon P. Chase for the Treasury, a Springfield friend gave him a hot tip: Chase liked telling people how he, Chase, was a bigger man than Lincoln.

"If you know of any other men who think they are bigger than I am," Lincoln replied, "let me know. I want to put them all in my Cabinet." Most people lacked the plain intellectual capacity to make Lincoln angry. He saw around, behind, and straight through nearly everyone and everything.

Donn Piatt knew well that Lincoln was no saint and admired him despite disapproving of some of Lincoln's casual, unpresidential ways. "We sat, far into the night, talking over the situation," Piatt wrote in describing a visit to the Lincoln residence in Springfield after the 1860 election.

> Mr. Lincoln was the homeliest man I ever saw. His body seemed to me a huge skeleton in clothes. Tall as he was, his hands and feet looked out of proportion, so long and clumsy were they . . . He sat with one leg thrown over the other, and the pendant foot swung almost to the floor. And for all the while, two little boys, his sons, clambered over those legs . . . without causing reprimand or even notice. He had a face that defied artistic skill to soften or idealize . . . It was capable of few expressions, but those were extremely striking.

Lincoln had promised to prevent the spread of slavery; he had *not* threatened to abolish it. He was determined to keep the United States together. Divorce would destroy the noblest, godliest experiment modern man had ever attempted. He did everything he could to sweet-talk the South into staying. His first inaugural address was dedicated to that purpose. "We are not enemies, but friends," he pleaded. "We must not be enemies." His despair is like a child's whose parents are bent on separating, on destroying the universe. Lincoln after all had made his career in the North but had been born in the South, in a slave state—although his family of course had owned no slaves. Lincoln was a child of the American Union. He was born when it was young. He loved and honored it like a devoted son. He could not and did not permit it to be destroyed.

But as soon as he was elected, southern states began to drop out. South Carolina seceded from the Union on November 17, 1860; Mississippi, Florida, Alabama, Georgia, Louisiana, and Texas followed in short order. Jefferson Davis was inaugurated President of the Confederacy two weeks before Lincoln himself was inaugurated in Washington. Sweet-talking the South was a lost cause. (In April 1861 Virginia would secede, followed by Arkansas, North Carolina, and Tennessee. But West Virginia broke away from Virginia and stayed in the Union.)

Lincoln's first inaugural address, in which he begged for reconciliation, centered on two of his favorite themes: peace and (to quote the title of the poem by Carl Sandburg) "The People, Yes!" (Sandburg published a multivolume Lincoln biography, arguably the best-loved Lincoln biography of them all.) Lincoln was elected as a "man of the people" and remained one as president. He was the least pompous of men, the least self-important. ("One summer morning," wrote Carpenter, "passing by the White

House at an early hour, I saw the President standing at the gateway, looking anxiously down the street; and, in reply to a salutation, he said, 'Good morning, good morning! I am looking for a newsboy; when you get to that corner, I wish you would start one up this way.' ") His belief in the people's wisdom, and in democracy itself, was deep and real and based on experience.

"While the people retain their virtue and vigilance," he said in that first inaugural, "no administration, by any extreme wickedness or folly, can very seriously injure the government in the short space of four years."

On April 12, 1861, the jarring thud of Confederate artillery opening on Fort Sumter before dawn meant that war was under way.

The earthquake of the Civil War relieved the enormous tensions that had been concentrated along the fault line (in a double sense) of slavery. The war left a relatively mature, stable Americanism behind. An Americanism that could look itself in the mirror without cringing. Yet there were bound to be more earthquakes. The war relieved huge built-up tensions, but no earthquake can repair or abolish the fault that let it (or made it) happen.

At the start the North fought for practical reasons: "The Union must be preserved." North and South will always be face-to-face, Lincoln said in that first inaugural; why should anyone believe that they would get along better as enemies than as friends? Midwesterners couldn't allow the Mississippi to fall into foreign hands; they needed their outlet to the sea. Workers hated the idea that free labor would be shut out of new territories by slavery. The moral issue was overshadowed at the start. But as the war continued, slavery itself emerged as *the* question, and the war's character changed. (Just as independence

emerged as the main issue only *after* the Revolutionary War had
begun.) Lincoln "knew that 'the plain people' were ready from
the first to fight in defense of the Union," wrote his friend
Brooks. "He knew that they were not at first ready to fight for
the destruction of slavery." But at length they became ready.

The North lost many battles in the early months. At last
Union forces under General George McClellan won the bloody
Battle of Antietam in September 1862. Soon afterward Lincoln
summoned his cabinet and announced his decision to issue the
Emancipation Proclamation. As of January 1, 1863, all slaves in
rebellious regions "shall be then, thenceforward, and forever
free." He saw the Proclamation as a first step; he believed that
his powers as president did not allow him to go farther than
freeing slaves in rebellious parts of the country. Eventually all
slaves would be freed by the Thirteenth Amendment of 1865.

Carpenter reported Lincoln's words at the crucial cabinet
meeting at which the Proclamation was announced. (Carpenter
had come to the White House later to make a painting of that
historic cabinet meeting, which he researched thoroughly.) "I
made a solemn vow before God," Lincoln said, "that if General
Lee was driven back from Pennsylvania, I would crown the result by the declaration of freedom to the slaves."

Public opinion on slavery had shifted; the question had become, when should Lincoln make this great announcement?
His decision reflected his relations with God as he understood
them. Antietam was a Union victory that stopped Lee's drive
north, for the time being. And in larger terms Lincoln believed
that the voice of the American people was the voice of the Lord.
The people's change of heart on slavery was a hint from God
that it was time to act.

But for Lee, Antietam was only a temporary reverse.

The Confederates marched north again. In the bloody three-day Battle of Gettysburg (July 1863), the Union stopped Lee's assault on Pennsylvania and halted the Confederate drive north for good. Lee withdrew toward the Shenandoah Valley. The day after Gettysburg, Grant captured Vicksburg on the Mississippi. The crisis had passed, the fever was broken, the delirium subsided; America was not going to die after all.

By the day on which Lincoln delivered his immortal speech at Gettysburg (November 19, 1863), almost no one doubted that the Union would win eventually. But at Gettysburg the fight had been close, and it could have gone either way. At the climax Lee had thrown fifteen thousand men into a mass assault across a shallow valley and up Cemetery Ridge. That last day had started bright and sunny in the green fields and rocky forests of southern Pennsylvania. As the men fought, it turned sweaty, grimy, and parched, smoky and stinking from gunfire, greasy with gore and blood. Lee and his men fought bravely but lost; they would never again threaten the North where it lived. The cost was enormous. Rebel losses reached 30,000 out of 70,000 men; the Union lost 23,000 out of roughly 90,000. Soon afterward a committee of northern governors organized a project to build a cemetery at the site. They invited the president, not expecting him to come. But he came.

In the Gettysburg Address Lincoln explained that the Union was fighting so "that this nation, under God, shall have a new birth of freedom." Once again, a *new birth*. The American Religion was created by three successive "new births": the Puritans arrived in the New World; America won her independence; America rededicated herself to her own ideals and took them seriously enough to free the slaves. Each of these three monumental events in world history illuminates the same biblical text: *Let my people go.*

The Emancipation Proclamation, which took effect in January 1863, changed the attitudes of many Europeans toward America. The Battle of Gettysburg did too. In the early part of the war Europe mostly supported the South. The European elite was scared of American radicalism and looked forward to the collapse of the great democratic experiment. France and even more Great Britain saw an independent Confederacy as the ideal trading partner—a supplier of raw materials and buyer of European manufactures, with no capacity to compete with the factories of Europe.

European attitudes to the United States during the Civil War are so enlightening that we can't pass by without listening in. It's impossible to understand Europe today without understanding Europe during the Civil War.

Listen to the diplomat and intellectual Henry Adams describe "the violent social prejudice" of British society against President Lincoln and Secretary of State Seward. (Adams, grandson of President John Quincy Adams, published his famous autobiography in 1918.) "London," he writes, "was altogether beside itself on one point, in especial; it created a nightmare of its own, and gave it the shape of Abraham Lincoln." (Compare this attitude to elite Europe's thoughts about Ronald Reagan or George W. Bush.) "Behind this it placed another demon, if possible more devilish, and called it Mr. Seward." (Just as Europe loved to hate former defense secretary Donald Rumsfeld and still loves to hate Vice President Dick Cheney.) "In regard of these two men, English society seemed demented. Defence was useless; explanation was vain; one could

only let the passion exhaust itself. One's best friends were as unreasonable as enemies, for the belief in poor Mr. Lincoln's brutality and Seward's ferocity became a dogma of popular faith."

The celebrated English novelist William Thackeray anguished
over the Union Army's treatment of his southern friends.

> In speaking of it, Thackeray's voice trembled and his eyes
> filled with tears. The coarse cruelty of Lincoln and his
> hirelings was notorious. He never doubted that the Feder-
> als made a business of harrowing the tenderest feelings
> of women—particularly of women—in order to punish
> their opponents. On quite insufficient evidence he burst
> into violent reproach.

Adams isn't describing rational beliefs or rational hatred.
Anti-American ideas are fervent, passionate, and violent, and
they are held as a matter of faith and not reason. We know that
Lincoln was *not* cruel, just as we know that Reagan was not and
Bush is not. But *something* must have caused these intense denunciations—a "something" that has nothing to do with American power or arrogance, or America pushing the world around,
or America refusing to give Europe its due, or America ignoring
the UN, or America polluting the globe. Because Adams reported denunciations that date from a time when America was
barely a second-rate power with *no* global presence, when none
of these Official American Sins had even been *conceived*.

Meanwhile the war dragged on.

In March 1864 Lincoln put Ulysses S. Grant in command of
all Union forces. Lincoln was renominated by the Republicans
for a second term in office—at last. Many wanted to dump him
in favor of a bolder, brasher, louder man. In September Sher-

man captured Atlanta for the Union. On November 8 Lincoln was reelected. Later that month Sherman started his march through Georgia to the sea.

In early March 1865 Lincoln was reinaugurated and delivered the Second Inaugural Address. On April 9 Lee surrendered to Grant at Appomattox Courthouse in Virginia.

Some 600,000 Americans had died. The painter Winslow Homer put the nation's feelings into one of the most haunting images in American art. *The Veteran in a New Field* (1865) shows a young man home at last from the war. He stands alone, his back to the viewer, in a wide wheat field under a quiet sky. He's busy at his work, bent to his task. The picture is softly silent and full of the blessed light of everyday normality. It's a picture of peace—of a nation tired of war and eager for its young men to be safely at home again; eager to forget. "They shall sit every man under his vine and under his fig tree; and none shall make them afraid" (Mic. 4:4). But it is also (as viewers saw from the first) a picture of death. The lone veteran swings a sickle as he reaps. Literally he is a brave and admirable young man. Symbolically he is the most accomplished veteran of all, the Grim Reaper, harvesting lives.

At war's end, on the night of Lincoln's last public address—April 11, 1865—there was a remarkable scene in Washington: all government buildings were lit up, including the brand-new dome atop Capitol Hill (an amazing achievement in the preelectric era). For a brief few moments the city's residents saw a powerful prophecy literally fulfilled. *Wee must Consider that wee shall be as a Citty upon a Hill, the eies of all people are upon us.* Winthrop had referred to the famous verse in Matthew (5:14): "Ye are the light of the world. A city that is set on an hill cannot be hid." America was indeed a shining city on a hill.

After Lincoln had proclaimed thanksgiving days in 1863 and 1864—specifying the last Thursday in November both times—Thanksgiving became a yearly custom. Puritanism and Americanism are both "available" to people of many denominations or faiths. Thanksgiving has the same characteristic: it is a religious festival that many faiths celebrate. Some historians have pointed out that the Puritans never held thanksgiving feasts on a fixed schedule; they celebrated when the Lord had blessed them. But often the Lord chastised them: the crops were bad, or hostile Indians threatened. On such occasions they did *not* celebrate. They held a fast, a "day of humiliation" and prayer to God.

A society that celebrates thanksgiving feasts on a fixed calendar has recognized its own steady, dependable success. Such ironic thanksgivings symbolize a community that no longer depends on God. That America's transition from irregular to fixed annual Thanksgiving days should be connected with Lincoln reflects several factors, including the reverence in which he himself was held and the deep confidence he inspired.

It also reflects a fundamental transition. *America was no longer a Puritan society.* The American Religion was poised to succeed Puritanism as the nation's "official" religion.

In Lincoln's last speech, four days before he was murdered, he proposed one more day of thanksgiving. An "immense throng" had gathered on the White House front lawn. "In the midst of this," he told them, "He from whom all blessings flow must not be forgotten. A call for national thanksgiving is being prepared."

He was murdered three days later. The Union was saved, slavery was on the way out (the Thirteenth Amendment had been proposed in January and was eventually to be ratified in December, 1865), Americanism was complete; and Lincoln was dead. He became not only the greatest preacher and prophet of this new American Religion, but its greatest martyr. He made Americanism holy. He became the perfect symbol of man reaching uncertainly but stubbornly and inexorably for the just, for the good, for the Lord.

America's Last and Greatest Founding Father

Lincoln's achievement was to complete the creation of an Americanism that was not mere patriotism, not mere philosophic doctrine, but a biblical religion in its own right.

How did Lincoln transform Puritanism into Americanism? I don't claim that he took explicit, deliberate steps to bring it about, only that his career contributed heavily to the metamorphosis.

We know two things to begin with: Puritanism inspired Lincoln; and in the years he was moving gradually but unstoppably toward the center of American history, Puritanism was dying.

We know that Lincoln tended to prefer the simpler varieties of Protestant Christianity, although it's unclear, as I've said, whether he actually considered himself a Christian. We know that Lincoln believed, as the Puritans did, in man's obligation to deal directly with the Bible and with God, one on one.

"I have felt His hand upon me in great trials," he said in June 1862, speaking of the Lord, "and submitted to His guidance, and I trust that as He shall further open the way I will be ready to walk therein, relying on His help and trusting in His goodness and wisdom." In 1863 he told one of his generals that "I locked the door, and got down on my knees before Almighty God, and prayed to him mightily for victory at Gettysburg. I told Him that this was His war, and our cause His cause."

Many thinkers have commented on Lincoln's sympathy for Puritan thinking. In his classic account of Lincoln's personal life (1922), Nathaniel Stephenson connects Lincoln with the leader of the Puritan forces in the seventeenth-century English Civil War and of the subsequent Puritan government: Oliver Cromwell. "Cromwell, in some ways, was undeniably his spiritual kinsman. In both, the same aloofness of soul, the same indifference to the judgments of the world, the same courage, the same fatalism, the same encompassment by the shadow of the Most High." In describing Lincoln's view of the war, the literary critic Edmund Wilson points out that "like most of the important products of the American mind at that time, it grew out of the religious tradition of the New England theology of Puritanism."*

Lincoln was deeply attached to the Bible. In 1864 he spoke of the Bible to his old friend Joshua Speed: "Take all of this Book upon reason that you can, and the balance on faith, and you will live and die a happier and better man." Isaac Arnold writes that Lincoln "knew the Bible by heart. There was not a clergyman to be found so familiar with it as he." "He would sometimes correct a misquotation of Scripture," writes Noah Brooks, "giving generally the chapter and verse where it could be found." He "liked the Old Testament best," Brooks adds. This predilection for the Hebrew Bible is another Puritan habit. Lincoln was said to be especially attached to Job and the Psalms.

Lincoln grew into an intensely religious man, although we rarely hear him described in those terms nowadays. His reli-

---

*Edmund Wilson, "Abraham Lincoln: The Union as Religious Mysticism," in *Eight Essays* (Garden City, N.Y.: Doubleday Anchor Books, 1954), p. 189.

gious faith became fundamental to his thinking and decision-making during the Civil War; we rarely hear that either. When he assumed the enormous burden of the presidency with war approaching, his faith grew deeper. When his beloved young son Willie died in early 1862, it deepened again—and seemed to continue growing deeper until his death. In the end Lincoln should almost certainly be remembered as the most important religious figure America has ever produced. I don't mean he was a theologian. But Amos, Isaiah, and Jeremiah weren't theologians either.

It seems also that the idea of a *covenant* or mutual vow between man and God was fundamental to Lincoln—and increasingly so as he got older. This bears again on the ways Lincoln was inspired by Puritanism. As I've noted, he told a cabinet meeting on a famous occasion in late September 1862 that he would issue the Emancipation Proclamation because "I made a solemn vow before God." When Antietam stopped Lee's drive north for the time being, Lincoln acted on his vow.

He objected to some aspects of Puritanism. He rejected the idea of eternal punishment; he seems to have rejected the idea of predestination. He seems also to have had doubts about the divinity of Jesus and the reality of the Trinity.

As for Puritanism itself, in the first part of the nineteenth century it was dying.

This is a complex story in its own right. Briefly, many leading Puritan churches in Boston—spiritual headquarters of American Puritanism—transferred their allegiance to Unitarianism. By 1800 *every* Boston church except one had a Unitarian preacher. The Harvard Divinity School was founded in 1816, essentially as a Unitarian institution. It became headquarters for

what the philosopher and essayist Ralph Waldo Emerson called
the "corpse-cold Unitarianism of Boston and Harvard College."

There's a revealing comment in Henry Adams's autobiography when he describes his first confrontation with slavery as a
teenager. With reference to that period—the mid-1800s—he
writes that "slavery drove the whole Puritan community back
on its Puritanism." No one could have written a thing like that
in 1630; the Puritan community had yet to wander *away* from
its Puritanism; it didn't have to be driven back. But in the mid-
1800s Puritanism was less a live religion than a recollected cultural attitude.

So we know that Puritanism influenced Lincoln; and we
know that when Lincoln became president, Puritanism was
dead or dying.

One other important thing about Lincoln: he exercised enormous moral authority. Naturally his authority grew during the
years of his presidency. It didn't hold everywhere or with everyone in the Union, but it was real and he knew it. His White
House secretary John Hay wrote that it was "absurd to call him
a modest man. No great man is ever modest." "There was something about Abraham Lincoln that enforced respect," Donn Piatt wrote. "No man presumed on the apparent invitation to be
other than respectful . . .

Through one of those freaks of nature that produce a
Shakespeare at long intervals, a giant had been born to the
poor whites of Kentucky, and the sense of superiority pos-
sessed President Lincoln at all times. Unobtruding and
even unassuming as he was, he was not modest in his assertion, and he as quietly directed Seward in shaping our
delicate and difficult foreign policy as he controlled Chase

in the Treasury and Edwin M. Stanton in the War Department. These men, great as they were, felt their inferiority to their master.

On a receiving line at a public reception in the White House, a man from Buffalo told the president, "Up our way we believe in God and Abraham Lincoln." Lincoln said, "My friend, you are more than half right."

In the fall of 1863, at a time when antiwar northern Democrats were attacking the Republicans and especially the president—Democrats who had once *supported* the war but had got tired of it—the *New York Times* came to the Republican president's defense. "In spite of all the hard trials and the hard words to which he has been exposed," the *Times* wrote, "Abraham Lincoln is today the most popular man in the Republic. All the denunciation and all the arts of the demagogue are perfectly powerless to wean the people from their faith in him."

A letter from a town in Massachusetts summarized the state of things at the end of his presidency. The letter was written on the day of his second inauguration. It starts by telling the president "how sorry we all are that you must have four years more of this terrible toil. But remember what a triumph it is for the right, what a blessing to the country . . . If you had been in this little speck of a village this morning, and heard the soft, sweet music of unseen bells rippling through the morning silence from every quarter of the far-off horizon, you would have better known what your name is to this nation." No more beautiful picture of America has ever been painted: the small town at the end of winter—March 4 was the date of the Second Inaugural—surrounded by wide, empty fields, a far-off horizon, and beyond, the ancient sturdy music of the bells "from every quarter," celebrating the reinauguration of Abraham Lincoln and the approaching end of a hard-fought, honorably won war.

In short, Lincoln's moral authority was enormous. Yet he did *not* join a church. On the other hand he once told a White House visitor, "I hope I am a Christian." And dozens of other comments bear on the topic. The question of Lincoln's relationship to Christianity is complex and subtle, but two things are clear. Although he went to church, he never joined one. Although he said nothing remotely disrespectful of Christianity—he congratulated the workers of Manchester, England, for example, on the "sublime Christian heroism" of their support of the Union cause—he never called *himself* a Christian plainly, publicly, unambiguously.

So what *did* he say? *What did he do* with his enormous moral authority? He might have been uncertain about Christianity, but he was never uncertain about America or Americanism.

We know that he was drawn as a youngish man to the idea of a "political religion," a term he used at age twenty-nine in an Illinois speech—by which he meant something like a "civil religion," a purely secular Americanism.

Much later, in the year (1858) of the Douglas debates, he used the phrase "my ancient faith" to refer not to Christianity or the Bible but to the Declaration of Independence. But when he let his love of country flow together with his devotion to God and the Bible, he arrived at a new and different kind of Americanism.

His first inaugural address concluded, "The mystic chords of memory, stretching from every battlefield and patriot grave to every living heart and hearthstone all over this broad land, will yet swell the chorus of the Union, when again touched, as surely they will be, by the better angels of our nature." No doubt he himself could hear those "mystic chords." They might have ushered in Lincoln's own deeper sense of Americanism as a full-fledged biblical religion.

He saw the principles of the Creed as derived from the Bible—not merely as "self-evident" truths.

He announced in 1858, as I have mentioned, that *equality* was a doctrine derived from the Bible. He understood *democracy* as the Lord's voice speaking through the people. "I must trust in that Supreme Being," he said, "who has never yet forsaken this favored land, through the instrumentality of this great and intelligent people." "Why should there not be a patient confidence in the ultimate justice of the people?" he asked; "is there any better, or equal hope, in the world?" And he made it clear many times as president that he saw *liberty* too as a gift of God. Thomas Jefferson had said that "the God who gave us life gave us liberty at the same time," and Lincoln clearly agreed. All three elements of the American creed—liberty, equality, democracy—came, for Lincoln, from the Bible and the Almighty.

His two greatest speeches are the center of America's own scriptures because of the light they throw on America and Americanism. The Declaration of Independence had been addressed to the world, especially the elite opinion-makers of Europe. In Lincoln's greatest speeches we hear America, after much pondering and suffering, addressing herself.

The Gettysburg Address of 1863 contains two kinds of statements: those that speak of the war and the great battle, and the two that restate the American Creed for all time. Those two being:

> Fourscore and seven years ago our fathers brought forth on
> this continent a new nation, conceived in liberty and dedi-

cated to the proposition that all men are created equal . . .
We here highly resolve that these dead shall not have died
in vain, that this nation under God shall have a new birth
of freedom, and that government of the people, by the
people, for the people shall not perish from the earth.

Thus *liberty*, *equality*, and *democracy*.

The speech is suffused with sanctity. The elements of the
Creed are lit up by the rest, which speaks of dedication, conse-
cration, devotion, hallowing: the Creed is presented in a sacred
setting, in a symbolic chapel built of suffering and sacrifice.

What Lincoln says in the Second Inaugural Address at the end
of his life is equally important to Americanism. His view of the
Civil War changed as the fighting continued. At the start he insisted that the war was strictly a fight to preserve the Union. Slavery was incidental. Personally he knew it to be evil: "If slavery is
not wrong, nothing is wrong," he said in 1854. But the Civil War
was a fight to determine—in his famous formulation—whether
a minority could do with bullets what it had failed to do with bal-
lots. Slavery was not at stake in the war as he first understood it.

But his opinion changed. The war, he came to believe, had
been imposed by God on a sinful nation. It's remarkable how
closely his explanation of the war in the Second Inaugural
matches the Puritan forecasts of John Winthrop about the
covenant community of America. Lincoln took the abstract, general formulations of Puritanism and fit them to American reality.

In 1630 Winthrop had written aboard the *Arabella*:

Thus stands the cause between God and us. Wee are entered into Covenant with him for this worke . . . If we shall

neglect the observation of these Articles... The Lord will surely *breake out in wrathe against us,* be revenged of such a perjured people and make us knowe the price of the breache of such a Covenant. [italics added]

Some 235 years later Lincoln spoke of particulars:

Yet if God wills that it continue, *until all the wealth piled by the bond-man's two hundred and fifty years of unre-quited toil shall be sunk, and until every drop of blood drawn with the lash, shall be paid by another drawn with the sword,* as was said three thousand years ago, so still it must be said: "the *judgments of the Lord are true and righteous altogether*" (Ps. 19:9). [italics added]

Lincoln has filled in the blanks in Winthrop's abstract indict-ment. Turning back to Winthrop (who alludes to Mic. 6:8):

Now the onely way to avoyde this shipwracke and to pro-vide for our posterity is to followe the Counsell of Micah, to doe Justice, to love mercy, to walke humbly with our God.

And Lincoln continued;

With Malice towards none; with charity for all; with firm-ness in the right, as God gives us to see the right, let us strive on to finish the work we are in.

Thus Lincoln devoted his greatest speech, at the end of his life, to explaining that the nation as a whole was guilty before the Lord and was punished by the Lord. It must devote itself now to *walking with* the Lord—to doing justice, loving mercy, and walking humbly with its God.

Of course, Lincoln didn't use the language of Puritanism. He did *not* speak of a covenant or a covenant community. He was inspired by Puritanism, but Puritanism was dead; instead he spoke the language of Americanism. When we compare Winthrop's words to Lincoln's, the transformation of Puritanism to Americanism shows up clearly.

Notice too that while Lincoln is telling us particulars about God and America, he has a broader message too, for every American forever. He could have left God out of the Second Inaugural, or soft-pedaled Him, or mentioned Him just in passing. He didn't. He put God right at the center of the most important speech he would ever give, the most widely read he would ever write. He did it deliberately, as he did everything. (His mind "worked slowly," Carpenter had written, "but strongly.") And it would have taken no genius to guess, with the war almost over and this speech almost certainly the last inaugural Lincoln would ever deliver (no president had held office for more than two terms), that this would be one of the most important speeches in American history. Lincoln rose to the occasion, as he had all his life.

Sorrow and grief had hollowed out a channel in Lincoln's life: the death of his two young boys, the war he couldn't prevent, the suffering and death all around him among the soldiers he visited often. The speech that came roaring down this channel like a river in spate defined Americanism for all time. To put it differently: the war and this great occasion created the mold, and Lincoln's speech filled it with the molten bronze of a new religion. Henceforth no man would ever be able to say that

Americanism was a civil or secular faith. Lincoln described his speech afterward in a letter to an admirer: "Men are not flattered by being shown that there has been a difference of purpose between the Almighty and them. To deny it, however, in this case, is to deny that there is a God governing the world." The greatest speech in American history was a sermon, pure and simple.

Lincoln's Second Inaugural is the exact center of American spiritual history. He could have delivered this address in church but chose not to; he could have delivered it to believing Christians only but did not. By speaking these words from the steps of the Capitol on democracy's most sacred occasion, he didn't Christianize America—he Americanized Christianity. He put Judeo-Christianity's holiest beliefs at America's disposal. He mixed them into the very concrete of which Americanism is made. (Modern leftists concede as much implicitly when they turn away from Americanism in disgust. After all, the American Creed is pure liberalism. But the Left knows, even if it won't admit it, that Americanism is a biblical religion—and the modern Left is fond of neither religion nor the Bible.)

"Both read the same Bible, and pray to the same God"—both the Union and the Rebels—

> and each invokes his aid against the other. It may seem strange that any men should dare to ask a just God's assistance in wringing their bread from the sweat of other men's faces; but let us judge not that we be not judged.*

*"Judge not, that ye be not judged" (Matt. 7:1; similarly, Luke 6:37). Compare the Talmud: "Do not judge your fellow man until you have been in his place" (Avot 3:5).

The prayers of both could not be answered; that of neither has been answered fully. The Almighty has His own purposes. "Woe unto the world because of offences! For it must needs be that offences come; but woe to that man by whom the offence cometh!"* If we shall suppose that American Slavery is one of those offences which, in the providence of God, must needs come, but which, having continued through His appointed time, He now wills to remove, and that He gives to both North and South, this terrible war, as the woe due to those by whom the offence came,† shall we discern therein any departure from those divine attributes which the believers in a Living God always ascribe to Him? Fondly do we hope—fervently do we pray—that this mighty scourge of war may speedily pass away. Yet, if God wills that it continue, until all the wealth piled by the bond-man's two hundred and fifty years of unrequited toil shall be sunk, and until every drop of blood drawn with the lash, shall be paid by another drawn with the sword, as was said three thousand years ago, so still it must be said "the judgments of the Lord, are true and righteous altogether."‡

With malice toward none; with charity for all; with firmness in the right as God gives us to see the right, let us strive on to finish the work we are in.

---

*"Woe unto the world because of offences! for it must needs be that offences come; but woe to that man by whom the offence cometh!" (Matt. 18:7).

†Lincoln holds North and South *equally* responsible for the sin of slavery.

‡"The judgments of the Lord are true and righteous altogether" (Ps. 19:9).

Lincoln tells us in this speech that discussion of God and the Bible *belongs* in America's public domain at the highest level, on the greatest occasion. Such discussion *is* America. It is what this nation is all about. He tells us implicitly, "Except the Lord keep the city, the watchman waketh but in vain" (Ps. 127:1). In America religion *must* be political, *is in fact* political; in America, religion concerns the citizen *and* the city. Religion is part of our history, identity, and future. Americanism is a biblical religion, just as surely as America herself is a biblical republic.

Lincoln addressed the doctrine of American Zionism too, in his own way, at other moments.

Of America he said, "I must trust in that Supreme Being who has never yet forsaken this favored land." If America is not a new promised land, it is at any rate a favored one—that the Lord has never yet forsaken.

Regarding Americans, he hoped to be a "humble instrument in the hands of the Almighty and of this, his almost chosen people." If Americans were not a new chosen people, they were at least—in his haunting phrase, which suggests (like a ship cutting through the water) progress toward a destination that has yet to be reached—an *almost* chosen people. He said that "we shall nobly save, or meanly lose, the last, best hope of earth"; if Americans were not the chosen people, their nation was at any rate the last, best hope.

And he told America: "Let us have faith that right makes might, and in that faith, let us, to the end, dare to do our duty as we understand it"—a view of Americanism as (potentially) a world religion with global responsibilities; a beautiful statement of the ideal of democratic chivalry.

On his way to Washington to assume the presidency, Lincoln had declared that America from its founding "held out a great promise to all the people of the world for all time to come." During that same trip he said that the Declaration of Independence gave "liberty, not alone to the people of this country, but hope to the world for all future time." The Declaration "gave promise that in due time the weights should be lifted from the shoulders of all men, and that *all* should have an equal chance." America had a mission to all mankind. Democratic chivalry was every American's duty.

Sometimes, in fact, Lincoln seems to be prophesying an Americanism that would actively promote the Creed all over the world. Of course he did not say that America must use military force to ensure "an equal chance" for all men. Such an idea would have been nonsense in 1861; America was no global power and had no global presence. We don't know how Lincoln would have acted in the twentieth century.

★   ★   ★

When Lincoln was murdered, the American Religion entered a new sphere of sanctity. After his death the *London Spectator* wrote that "we cannot read" the Second Inaugural Address "without a renewed conviction that it is the noblest political document known to history, and should have for the nation and the statesmen he left behind him something of a sacred and almost prophetic character. Surely, none was ever written under a stronger sense of the reality of God's government."

"We hear Lincoln's words in every school-house and college," Isaac Arnold wrote in his 1884 Lincoln biography, "in every cabin and at every public meeting. We read them in every newspaper, school-book and magazine . . . His words, becoming some of them as familiar as the Bible, are on the tongues of all the people, shaping the national character."

Lincoln's martyrdom was a human catastrophe and a political one. But in religious terms, it sealed his achievement.

And here is the remarkable final chapter: at the end of his life he had told his inner circle that, in effect, he could see death coming. His martyrdom was approaching, and he knew it. How did he tell people, and why?

He told them by recounting a dream and reciting a passage from Shakespeare.

He reported the uncanny dream only days before his death. He had seen a crowd hurrying to the White House. When he followed it to the East Room—he mentioned the East Room specifically—he heard voices repeating "Lincoln is dead," and found his own corpse laid out. On April 9, 1865, only five days before he was murdered, as he traveled by steamship from Grant's headquarters back to Washington, he read aloud a passage from *Macbeth*: "Duncan is in his grave; / After life's fitful fever he sleeps well; / Treason has done his worst: nor steel, nor poison, / Malice domestic, foreign levy, nothing, / Can touch him further."

During his last days in a turbulent, tipsy, crowded, jubilant, and dangerous city he knew he was looking death in the face, that he would die soon. He knew it, but why say so? What was his purpose?

Many years later, Harry Truman made a strange statement in a speech after he left office: "Yes, I am Cyrus." Cyrus in the Bible is the Persian king who restores the Jews to their homeland. Truman was commenting on his role in the creation of the modern state of Israel. Lincoln made a similar statement, implicitly: "Yes, *I am Moses.*" God told Moses that he would never reach the promised land, though he had struggled toward it his whole life. He would never reach it, but in recompense he would *know* it, with the Lord as his guide. God showed him the whole land from the mountaintop before he died.

Lincoln devoted his last days to urging reconciliation between South and North, to repeating the pleading message with which his first inaugural address had concluded: "We are not enemies, but friends. We must not be enemies." In his last public address he said of the southern states that "finding themselves safely at home, it would be utterly immaterial whether they had ever been abroad. Let us all join in doing the acts necessary to restoring the proper practical relations between these states and the Union." The speech did not go down well. The crowd wanted revenge. On the last full day of his life he pardoned a deserter and revoked the death sentence of a Confederate spy. (He had issued innumerable pardons and commuted innumerable death sentences all through his presidency.) He called a cabinet meeting. He spoke generously of Lee and other Confederate officers— and even more so of the rank and file of the Confederate army.

But the North was in no mood to forgive. And with Lincoln gone, Reconstruction was a disaster. Lincoln had said only *listen*, for your own good—*listen to the words of a dead man*, martyred (or about to be!) for his country and his people; I can see just where we are going, and when I die that will be your sign that I told the truth, listen *please*; but no one would.

And today we ignore him again—and relive Reconstruction in our own small (small!) way.

The Confederates championed an evil cause. Slavery was a foul sin; we have no right to forgive them. But men like Stonewall Jackson and Robert E. Lee had more than enough nobility of character to justify any American child's (black or white) knowing and admiring them. They were *more* than the sum of their sins—just as we hope to be! "There stands Jackson

like a stone wall!——rally behind the Virginian!" Every American schoolboy used to thrill to those words, if only momentarily.
Today most of our schools seem to teach *no* good about the
South or its leaders. *We are not enemies, but friends. We must not
be enemies.* Once again Lincoln pleads and America won't listen.

The same holds on the largest scale. Lincoln told us to deal
generously and in brotherhood with the South after the war, so
how should we deal with America *itself*? The United States has
committed sins throughout its history. And many schools nowadays seem to teach those sins exclusively, as if the nation had
done nothing else. Many American children nowadays find patriotism either laughable or incomprehensible. That is what
they have been taught. *We are not enemies, but friends. We must
not be enemies.* Too many of our cultural leaders can't seem to be
friends with their own countrymen even with no civil war to
contend with. "It's getting awfully easy to hate this country,"
said that Ivy League professor not terribly long ago.

According to Noah Brooks, when Lincoln addressed the
crowd in the lit-up city of Washington on April 11, 1865——two
days after the surrender at Appomattox, four days before the
murder——he did indeed seem like Moses, looking "into the
promised land of peace from the Pisgah summit." Brooks knew,
deeply, what he was talking about.

And what should we say about Lincoln in the end?

He poured his whole passion for God and the Bible into
Americanism. He proclaimed Americanism a world religion.

His extraordinary personality made Americanism live. His
martyrdom made it holy.

★ ★ ★

The last photo dates from April 9, 1865. Lee had surrendered
that morning, but no triumph or even relief is evident in Lin-

coln's portrait. The knit-together eyebrows, worried forehead, and vastly tired eyes seem puzzled by a strange conundrum, one he has pondered so long it is marked on his face. His haphazard bow tie is off center. The worn skin is coarse as sandpaper. Of all the faces that have ever been captured in photographs, his may be the one with the greatest capacity to occasion gratitude and love.

F. B. Carpenter wrote, "It has been the business of my life to study the human face, and I have said repeatedly to friends that Mr. Lincoln had the saddest face I ever attempted to paint." Lincoln was unsophisticated, unpretentious, and astonishingly eloquent—only Shakespeare had a more perfect gift for the right word (and naturally Lincoln loved Shakespeare and re-cited long passages by heart). Lincoln was close to man, close to God, deeply loved—deeply hated; Lincoln's face is America's face. What a beautiful face it is.

CHAPTER 6

THE GREAT WAR
MAKES THE MODERN WORLD

T he First World War was a crisis for America, Americanism, and the whole wide world. America made an enormously ambitious push toward democratic chivalry and the worldwide realization of the American Creed—and the confirmation of "I believe in America" as a global statement of faith and hope. America's participation in World War I was her attempt to act like the new chosen people, to set forth on a chivalrous quest to perfect the world; to spread liberty, equality, and democracy to all mankind.

But the result of America's plan was merely a partial success. The outcome of the Great War itself was a tragedy that is still with us: a world shivered into three dangerous jagged fragments: descendants of the winners who still feel guilty, descendants of the losers who still feel resentful, and the United States, which managed (miraculously) to fight and win yet *not* be permanently injured. For this we are still blamed by the guilty winners and resentful losers. American intellectuals felt cheated; they wanted their own ghastly, futile great war to make Americans, too, sick at the very *idea* of war. They tried to force Vietnam into that mold—and succeeded.

Still, Woodrow Wilson's plan started America thinking. "It was our duty to go in," Wilson wrote after the war was over, "if we were indeed the champions of liberty and right." (If we were *indeed* chivalrous knights of the American Creed.) "We answered to the call of duty in a way so spirited, so utterly without thought of what we spent of blood or treasure . . . that the whole world saw at last, in the flesh, in noble action, a great ideal asserted and vindicated." When the Soviet Union reared up after World War II, to issue a challenge conveyed in bloody deeds and not words—*we will take and tyrannize* in the name of our insatiable lust for security *as much of the world as we can get*— Wilsonian America was ready. Wilson's vision, and Lincoln's, and Winthrop's, had *made* America ready. She stepped forth as the leader and defender of the free world. The noble knight rode forth at last, and Americanism was at last a true world religion.

Wilson was not a man of Lincoln's stature. But he was a principled and profoundly Christian man who worked hard to keep America out of the First World War, as Lincoln had tried to avoid a civil war; who insisted, as Lincoln had, that the United States must fight for her principles and not just her interests; who sought a peace of reconciliation with the beaten enemy, as Lincoln had—and failed to achieve it, as Lincoln (through no fault of his own) had also failed. After the armistice in November 1918 Wilson traveled to Europe to attend the Paris Peace Conference; he was greeted by cheering throngs in France, England, and Italy. But it was clear on his return to the United States in June 1919 that it wouldn't be easy to win Senate acceptance of the peace treaty that had been negotiated in Paris and that included provision for a League of Nations.

Wilson regarded the creation of the League as crucial to the treaty and the future peace of the world. But anti-internationalist Republicans had won control of the Senate in November 1918—and Wilson dealt with them tactlessly, foolishly. On his return from Europe he set off on a country-wide tour to build public support for the treaty and the League. He collapsed in September 1919 and returned to Washington incapacitated. As soon as he had partially recovered, he resumed trying to win Senate support for the treaty—or enough public support to compel Senate support. But in March 1920 the Senate refused to ratify. (Wilson could have won ratification and American participation in the League, but only under conditions and restrictions that were unacceptable to him.) So America never did join the League of Nations that Wilson had done so much to create.

Activist, Wilsonian Americanism did not insist that the United States must send in the marines to knock down every tyrant everywhere. (Somehow the word *activist* seems to apply nowadays mainly to liberals. But Wilson's foreign policy was obviously activist, and so is George W. Bush's.) The president's first duty is to keep America safe. But every tyrant is a potential danger to America. To make war on America is irrational. But it is comparatively easy for a tyrant to act irrationally; he is answerable to almost no one. It is harder for democratically elected politicians to do the same; they must answer to voters.

America's safety depends, furthermore, on her good name—among other things. If her reputation suffers, if people doubt she is tough enough to win *every* war, including long, hard, bitter ones, her safety suffers. She is more likely to be attacked.

September 11 came shortly after the close of eight Democratic years. Of course the Democrats didn't *cause* 9/11; but their foreign policy did little to discourage the mass murderers who thought it up. Wilsonian Americanism requires finely balanced decision-making—but insists that *spreading the Creed to all mankind* must never be far from America's thoughts.

And whenever self-defense *forces* America to fight, *she must fight for her principles, not only for her interests.* This is the essence of activist Americanism. America must make the most of any war into which she is forced. She must use the evil of war to spread the good of liberty, equality, democracy. If she is *not* forced to fight, she must use all her resources short of war-making to help the oppressed and spread the Creed.

President Wilson preached an active, chivalrous, global Americanism. In the short term, his idea didn't take; when World War I was over, the United States shut the windows, pulled down the shades, and went back to sleep. (Wake us at the next global crisis.) Traditional American isolationism returned. In the long term, however, the questions posed by Wilson's vision have dominated the last century of American foreign policy. Wilson made important contributions to Americanism, and the nasty reaction to Wilson—especially among European intellectuals—set modern anti-Americanism on its own powerful course. The antagonists were made for each other, like a batter's strong swing and a smoking fastball.

Although World War I strikes some people as ridiculously obscure, it was vital to the development of America and Americanism. To see why, ponder a less obscure topic: the Vietnam War Memorial in Washington. Just about every living American has seen the Vietnam Wall or photos of it. It is every bit as famous as World War I is obscure—to use a strange analogy that is not really so strange—because the black wall and the Great War are intimately related.

Some Americans wrongly suppose that Maya Lin, designer of the Vietnam Wall, invented the idea of focusing a memorial on the names of the dead. But the Wall is novel mainly insofar as it buries the honored names in a ditch (meant to suggest a wound or scar); that *is* novel. Not for nothing is this the favorite war memorial of America's cultural elite. It mourns dead soldiers without honoring or thanking them. But in listing every name, it resembles many famous European memorials to the casualties of World War I. In Louvencourt, for example, the names of dead German soldiers appear in raised metal characters against somber black stone. Monuments all over Europe list dead men's names one by one by one by one. At Gallipoli a huge broken obelisk bears the names of Allied dead. At Ypres the overwhelming Menin Gate carries the names of 54,365 British or British Empire soldiers who went missing in nearby battles. (This figure is close to the total on the Vietnam Wall.) The most celebrated memorial is the Thiepval Arch at the Somme battlefield by the great English architect Sir Edwin Lutyens, where 73,357 names are listed.

The resemblance between America's Vietnam Memorial and Europe's memorials to soldiers of the Great War is deeply appropriate even if it happened by accident. *Vietnam was America's Great War*, its World War I. Vietnam made pacifism and appeasement the religion of America's cultural elite, just as the Great War did in western Europe. World War I is the most important event in modern history, not just politically and pragmatically but intellectually. Ever since World War I intellectuals have attempted to squeeze *every* war into this mold. Wars that fit have been rewarded with enormous cultural influence. Nowadays liberal intellectuals try to squeeze Iraq into the Vietnam mold, or more precisely the Vietnam-as-they-see-it mold. In doing so, they are really trying to squeeze it (indirectly) into the World War I mold.

World War I is hugely important today for another reason as well. In today's world the fashionable attitudes and major intellectual movements are ones that emerged in the period *following World War I.* Between that era and today stands the colossus of World War II. But when the Cold War ended, World War II vanished like dirty fog from the world landscape; it dissipated like the smoke of Auschwitz, which the world longs to forget. Pacifism and appeasement are strong today in Europe, *as they were in the years following World War I.* The map of Europe is clogged with small states, *as it was following World War I.* States created after World War I and submerged after World War II have floated back to the surface, like buoyant objects artificially pinned to the bottom for two generations. I will return to this observation.

In short, World War I is important for many reasons. And all these reasons are present implicitly in the fact that the Great War introduced an argument about Americanism—should it be passive or active?—that is still raging.

I will discuss Americanism in the era before the Great War; then (in outline) the war itself and Wilson's role; then the Great War's consequences for the world today; and in conclusion Wilson's view of the American Religion.

Prelude to Activist Americanism

The murder of Lincoln was crucial to the development of the American Religion. Mature Americanism bloomed in the late nineteenth century.

Where did Americanism stand *before* Lincoln and the Civil

War? It was an unformed religion—naturally, because it was brand-new. Before the Civil War, Puritanism remained the country's dominant spiritual influence—outside the intellectual elite, which had moved toward Unitarianism and related movements. In mainstream America, Puritanism was dominant in the first part of the nineteenth century, not in the sense that most Americans were practicing Puritans but insofar as Americans thought of Puritan Christianity as the main source of the country's values and outlook.

Consider *The American Orator; or Elegant Extracts in Prose and Poetry*, published in 1811. This manual for budding orators and statesmen includes such milestone texts as "Washington's speech to the first congress" and "Extracts from Washington's farewell." But the sections that deal with Americans and Americanism are dominated by the many pages on Christianity. "Eloquence of the Pulpit" is the longest chapter in the book. Books like this one suggest that Christianity with a Puritan flavor continued to dominate the nation's spiritual life.

Or consider *The American Manual*, assembled and published by Moses Severance in 1849, "consisting of exercises in reading and speaking ... selected from the best writers." Most of the writers are British. The first short piece by an American appears toward the end of chapter 3 and is called "Religion the only basis for society." That was a quintessentially American attitude at the time.

Severance's chapter on "public speeches" is noteworthy. It contains no speeches by Washington, Jefferson, Patrick Henry, or anyone else from the revolutionary generation. The brief closing section on American history is detached and low key. Americanism was still an immature adolescent, unsure of itself.

Or consider *Essays to Do Good* by the eminent Cotton Mather, a collection of aphorisms for everyday life. It was first published in 1710, long before independence, but was republished with minor changes and updates in 1826. In other words, Puritan guides to living still found buyers well into the nineteenth century. "Between 1650 and 1775 there was far more change in the temper of England," remarked an English historian,* "than in that of America." At the time of the Revolution, Americans were still under the influence of seventeenth-century Puritan ideas. This conservative cultural bent continued to be important for the next seventy-five years. The American Religion was solid and sturdy and grew slowly, like a New England sugar maple.

But Abraham Lincoln and the Civil War worked a fundamental transformation. America emerged as *something to believe in,* a spiritual concept to have faith in just as you might believe in Christianity.

Why did the transformation happen? It was under way before Lincoln became president, but after the Civil War Americanism had a new maturity, vividness, and spiritual depth.

Three facts combined were immensely potent. The Union had passed through bitter suffering to win the Civil War and free the slaves. Lincoln had spoken unforgettably about America and Americanism. And he had died a martyr, sanctifying the American Religion and lifting it to transcendent heights. Recall Isaac Arnold: as of 1884, Lincoln's best-known words were "as familiar as the Bible."

America was maturing as a theological concept. The distin-

*Barrett Wendell, "The American Intellect," in *The Cambridge Modern History,* vol. 7, *The United States* (Cambridge: Cambridge University Press, 1934), p. 724.

guished liberal rabbi Isaac Mayer Wise said so clearly. Four years after Lincoln's death he gave a speech in which he summarized Americanism as he saw it and as Lincoln had shaped it. He had been asked, Wise said, to address "a subject dear and precious to all of us, our country, our promised land, the home and fortress of freedom, the blessed spot which flows with milk and honey, upon which we invoke God's gracious blessing."* Belief in America meant belief in a new *promised land*, flowing (naturally!) with milk and honey. And America was *the home and fortress of freedom*. Both the Creed and American Zionism are part of Wise's statement.

Writing in 1896, the Irish historian William Lecky summarized in *Democracy and Liberty* the transformation wrought by Lincoln and the war. America's national character, Lecky wrote, "was especially admirable in the very trying moments that followed the assassination of Lincoln." Lecky saw the murder of Lincoln as a hinge between two drastically different images of America. Once Europe had dismissed the United States as unimportant. No more. "America rose at this time," at the murder of Lincoln, "to a new place and dignity in the concert of nations. Europe had long seen in her little more than an amorphous, ill-cemented industrial population. It now learned to recognise the true characteristics of a great nation."

At the end of the century the British historian and member of Parliament James Bryce discussed Americanism in *The American Commonwealth* (1898). America's Constitution "forms the

---

*Isaac M. Wise, "Our Country's Place in History," in Conrad Cherry, *God's New Israel: Religious Interpretations of American Destiny* (Englewood Cliffs, N.J.: Prentice-Hall, 1971), p. 218.

mind and temper of the people," Bryce wrote. "It makes them feel that to comprehend their supreme instrument of government is a personal duty, incumbent on each one of them. It familiarizes them with, it attaches them by ties of pride and reverence to, those fundamental truths on which the Constitution is based." Notice the religious undertone. He is describing not just patriotism or civic pride but *Americanism,* the American Religion.

There is only a short hop from Bryce's statement to the "charming youth" who recited the Declaration to Rupert Brooke a couple of years before World War I. Woodrow Wilson summarized the newly emerged religion: "I believe that the glory of America is that she is a great spiritual conception . . . The one thing that the world cannot permanently resist," he continued, "is the moral force of great and triumphant convictions." And: "America came into existence, my fellow citizens, in order to show the way to mankind in every part of the world to justice, and freedom, and liberty." *To show the way, in every part of the world:* activist Americanism.

This was Americanism as a world religion—for the oppressed, the persecuted, and the simply idealistic all over the globe.

The Making of Woodrow Wilson

Wilson has nothing like Lincoln's epochal importance to Americanism and world history. But few men do. Wilson's significance is real, and his importance great. We don't need his story in detail, but we do need the high points.

He was born in 1856 in Staunton, Virginia, but the family soon moved to Georgia. Lincoln figured in one of his earliest memories, of a man shouting, "Lincoln is elected and now we will have war."

Wilson was the son and grandson of Presbyterian ministers. His Presbyterian upbringing shows through his thought and writing as plainly as pebbles at the bottom of a clear mountain stream. Among the speeches of American presidents, only Lincoln's are more biblical. Throughout his life Wilson was in the habit of reading the Bible and praying every day. Soon after World War I began in Europe, he designated one Sunday as "a day of prayer and supplication" and requested "all God-fearing persons to repair on that day to their places of worship, there to unite their petitions to Almighty God that . . . He vouchsafe his children healing peace." Wilson was deeply religious and talked like that all the time.

At seventeen he departed for the staunchly Presbyterian Davidson College. Toward the end of his first year he got sick and went home, where he had to stay for the next two winters. Recovered at last, he returned to Princeton instead of Davidson. Princeton had once been a Presbyterian school itself, but its main mission by the time Wilson arrived was to educate the sons of the upper class.

After Princeton he studied law at the University of Virginia, and he practiced briefly. But he was drawn to politics; he was a talented politician—and a born intellectual also. An odd combination. But Wilson's archrival Teddy Roosevelt was also a natural writer and something of a scholar, among many other things. Roosevelt seemed warm, vibrant, and likable, even lovable; Wilson seemed cold and distant and abstract. They make a striking pair, moving through American history like an image and its photo negative—in some ways identical, in others nearly opposite. There is no word for this kind of pair, but I call them *countertypes*. Wilson gave up lawyering to work toward his doctorate in political science at Johns Hopkins. In 1890 he was appointed professor of political science at Princeton; twelve years later he became Princeton's president.

Today's American universities are widely criticized as unrepresentative because their faculties are overwhelmingly left-wing and the country isn't. Wilson attacked an earlier version of the same problem. Princeton was unrepresentative because it catered (or toadied) to the upper class. "The American college must become saturated in the same sympathies as the common people," Wilson said. (Good luck.) "The colleges of this country must be reconstructed from the top to the bottom. The American people will tolerate nothing that savours of exclusiveness." He wasn't kidding, but he might as well have been.

In 1910 he became the Democratic nominee for governor of New Jersey and was duly elected. In 1912 a bitterly embattled Democratic convention nominated him for president—on the forty-sixth ballot. In November Wilson faced *two* Republican incumbents. He beat President William Howard Taft and the pre-Taft incumbent and far more popular Theodore Roosevelt, who was running as the Progressive Party candidate. Roosevelt had resigned from politics at the end of his second term in 1909. But he was so unhappy with the performance of his picked successor, Taft, that he got back in—and got beaten by Taft for the 1912 Republican nomination. (The party big shots were against him.) But Roosevelt refused to withdraw. He went down fighting. All in all, 1912 was one of strangest, noisiest years in American political history.

For many decades Woodrow Wilson has almost universally been regarded as a naïve, self-righteous failure. But his reputation is coming around. He *was* naïve and self-righteous; in some ways he was a failure. Yet it seems unfair that his ideas should be so much more fashionable nowadays than he is: democracy, freedom, and self-determination, the rights of small states, international politics conducted openly and ethically, and foreign policies devoted to making the world better. George W. Bush is a student of Wilson and shares his idealism, his piety, and his gift for being hated. But Wilson was a cold fish, famously unable to pass himself off as a human being. Bush is friendly, warm, charmingly open, and slightly defensive—just as Americans are traditionally thought to be. Henry James could have invented George W. Bush. Bush is even rich; James liked that in an American character.

Wilson piloted America successfully through the Great War, all things considered. But naturally the war took its tragic toll on America as it did on every other combatant nation.

The War to End War

In World War I, which lasted from 1914 to 1918, each major European power took body blow after body blow and kept on fighting. The European victors of the First World War emerged in strutting-proud condition, but that was only a facade. The proud fronts that Britain and France showed at the peace conference of 1919 were like the facades of bombed-out buildings, seemingly whole but ready to topple on their faces in the first stiff breeze.

America entered the fighting during its final months and suffered 115,000 dead or wounded. "Your war, our dead," Americans might have shouted at Europe—but didn't. In fact, "Your war, our dead" was written on a protestor's banner at an anti–Iraq war rally in Rome in 2004.

American casualties in the Great War sound enormous and were. But the British Empire suffered close to a million casualties, France a million and a quarter, Russia and Germany roughly 1.7 million each. In one great offensive, on the Somme in France, Britain suffered *sixty thousand* killed, wounded, or captured—on the first day. Few catastrophes are harder to comprehend than the Great War.

In 1914 there were plenty of thoughtful statesmen who did not want war and did what they could to forestall it. By the late nineteenth century Europeans seemed to have mastered the art of keeping war clear of Europe and restricted to remote colonial outposts. Many wealthy and middle-class Europeans understood how good they had it and had no wish to run risks. Only days before war began, Britain's prime minister—the formidably brilliant and scholarly, the supremely articulate, upright, and liberal, the eloquent, patronizing, detached, and ever-so-slightly boring Herbert Henry Asquith—noticed that the "desire to keep out at almost any cost" was gaining ground among influential Britons.* So what happened? Why did war come anyway?

Question number one—how did it all begin?—is easier to answer than is sometimes made out. The war started because the German general staff had a neat plan to smash France— such a surefire, wonderful plan that they were burning, itching, *dying* to try it out.

There were many rivalries in early-twentieth-century Europe, but none so dangerous as that between Germany and France. Enmity between the two went back centuries. Their last full-scale bout, the Franco-Prussian War of 1870, had been provoked by Paris and Berlin jointly—one of the few projects on which they had ever collaborated. Only in modern times have the French and Germans become friends, to the tune of

*Roy Jenkins, *Asquith* (London: Collins, 1965), p. 326.

their shared dislike of Britain and detestation of America. Not by accident, a German philosopher—albeit an *anti-German* German, Friedrich Nietzsche—built much of his philosophy around an analysis of resentment, Germany's quasi-official national emotion—just as guilt belongs to England, smugness to France, and piety to America.*

Now Germany had a wonderful new plan to smash France, the Schlieffen plan. This plan, which was burning a hole in Germany's pocket, was the single most important fact in the whole wide world at the start of fatal, fateful 1914. In a certain sense it was the decisive fact of the whole twentieth century.

The Schlieffen plan called for Germany to come down on France like a sledgehammer. The German army would pound hard from the north and smash France on the head. But Germany is *east* (not north) of France, so the hammer head of the German army would pivot through Belgium to strike France from above. The stationary pivot point was south, near the Swiss border. The hammer head would swing around through Belgium, come down on France, and keep swinging. The French army would be sent reeling south and east, to be crushed against the Swiss border like a sailing ship driven by mighty waves into a lethal crag. *In six weeks*, said the brisk, heel-clicking German generals in their spike-decorated clown hats, *France's goose will be cooked*—and then Germany could turn her attention east and smash Russia! The Reich, by the way, would hold on to Belgium forever for the sake of her Atlantic ports, which were well to the west of Germany's own.

The only fly in the Schlieffen-plan ointment was that Britain

*Such generalizations should never be taken too seriously; just seriously enough.

had promised to protect Belgium. Britain, France, and Prussia had guaranteed Belgium neutrality ever since the modern Belgian state was created in 1839. (Prussia's having been one of the guarantors of Belgian freedom did not interest the Germans.) On August 2, 1914, Germany told Belgium that she must let German troops march through on the way to France, must let that hammer head *swing*; otherwise Belgium would be treated as an enemy of the German Reich. Belgium refused. Invasion followed as promised. Two days later Britain declared war on Germany. From 1914 until the war's end, all of Belgium but the northwestern corner was occupied by the Imperial German Army.

Had Germany attacked France *without* violating Belgium, Britain might well have stayed out—and the war and the world would have been oh-so-very different.

Look at Europe on the brink of the First World War: the map is startling. It is so *simple*. Continental Europe consisted mainly of France, the Low Countries, Italy—and three huge empires: Germany, Russia, and Austria-Hungary. There was no Poland or Czechoslovakia (or Czech Republic or Slovakia); no Hungary or Finland, no Latvia or Estonia or Lithuania, no Ukraine or Belarus . . .

This simple, elegant map was shattered like a magnificent picture window in June 1914 by a Bosnian terrorist who hurled a rock through it, by shooting and killing the heir to the Austro-Hungarian throne. Serbia, a state sponsor of terrorism, helped plan and underwrite the murder, and Austria knew it. (Bosnia was part of Austria-Hungary, but Serbia was an independent state.) Austria-Hungary raged against Serbia and tried to decide what to do.

She consulted her friend Germany. Germany urged her to go right ahead and smash Serbia if she felt like it. On the topic of smashing undersize neighbors, Germans were always sympathetic. Austria-Hungary declared war on Serbia. Serbia meanwhile was counting on Russia for help against Austria. Russia was counting on France.

So Russia mobilized her gigantic, dim-witted army, like a dinosaur with shark's teeth, alligator's claws, and a pea-sized brain, but not *only* against Austria—against Germany too. It was a profoundly stupid mistake. Germany demanded an end to Russia's anti-German mobilization. Russia refused, and so Germany declared war on Russia (August 1) and on Russia's ally France (August 3). Notice that all three great hulking eastern empires were committed to war before a single western European democracy took the plunge. It is fatally easy for a dictator to make war.

As for England, she had no formal alliance with any European combatant. But she had an informal understanding with France and had promised to protect Belgium. When the Germans crashed into Belgium like a rogue elephant into a child's lemonade stand, Britain declared war on Germany.

Nowadays Americans often think of the First World War, to the extent they think about it at all, as a tragedy of errors, a catastrophic piece of silliness. This view is simple-minded.

Belgium and France were attacked and had to defend themselves. Britain's declaration of war turned the fight into a *world* war—and Britain declared war to do her duty by Belgium, which she had promised to defend. Britain acted out of loyalty—and on behalf of the independence of small states, of international trust and international law, and of her own traditional policy of preventing any one power from dominating continental Europe.

Did Britain act selflessly? No; no nation ever does or ever can. But she acted carefully, for good reasons, and for the good of the international community as well as her own. When Americans entered the war three years later, they did it carefully too. Americans believed they were fighting "the war to end war," a war "to make the world safe for democracy." It would be a war to protect freedom of the seas and to repay a debt we had owed France ever since Lafayette and the American Revolution. Americans were naïve and noble—as usual at key moments in American history.

At the very start the Japanese (who had been associated with Britain by treaty since 1902) declared war on Germany and overran German holdings in China. The Japanese onslaught in China was a foretaste of the Second World War.

Eventually many others joined the fight. Turkey declared war on Russia (1914); Bulgaria declared war on Serbia (1915); and Italy, on account of lavish bribes offered secretly by Britain and France, attacked Austria (1915).

Germany had the bright idea that she could make trouble for her enemies by fomenting rebellion. Ireland was still ruled by Britain, so Germany landed an Irish nationalist by U-boat. With the aid of other Irish nationalists and German agents, he caused an enormous uproar and got several people hanged. The 1916 Easter Rebellion against Britain, which inspired Yeats to write one of the great poems of the twentieth century, was duly put down.

In January 1917 German diplomats had another brainstorm: they would send Mexico a secret message offering her big chunks of former Mexican territory that had been incorporated since the 1840s into the United States—Texas, New Mexico, Arizona—*if* the United States should declare war on Germany *and* Mexico should then come in on the German side. The British intercepted this message, decoded it, and handed it to Washington. Before long it appeared in U.S. newspapers. The proposal was hilarious, but Americans did not see the humor in it at the time. (To be fair, President Wilson showed a similar level of diplomatic finesse during and after the Paris Peace Conference at the end of the war.)

At the war's start, the British navy blockaded Germany. Germany tried to return the favor by launching an all-out U-boat campaign against military *and* civilian ships. In 1915 a German U-boat torpedoed the British liner *Lusitania*. Among the twelve hundred drowned were more than one hundred Americans.

The United States was outraged. Germany backed down rather than risk an American declaration of war. She called off unrestricted U-boat warfare. She did not want to fight the United States if she could help it. In November 1916 Wilson was reelected on a peace platform—"He kept us out of war" was the campaign slogan, highly effective. But in early 1917 Germany, feeling pressed, resumed all-out U-boat warfare— and in April 1917 Wilson went to Congress and got a declaration of war against Germany and her allies, mainly because of German U-boat attacks on American and other neutral ships; but that message to Mexico helped too. Of course Wilson's deeper goals had to do with Americanism, with American principles rather than American interests.

And that is, briefly, why the major combatants fought. But *how* did they fight?

The war was fought by opposing armies ankle deep, waist deep, chest deep in an ever-rising sea of blood. We must grasp

166 AMERICANISM

this ghastly reality, or we will never understand the modern world, modern Americanism, *or* anti-Americanism.

One side set up a wall of machine-gun bullets and the other walked right into it and died, or (to put it differently) walked *through* it and came out dead and marched onward—legions of ghosts to haunt the Continent forever. On the Western Front, where France, England, Belgium, and later America struggled with Germany, trench warfare prevailed: this was the first European war to be fought with machine guns. The only way to protect yourself against the machine gun was to dig in, or—where the ground was too wet—to build sandbag fortifications. World War I was the trench war. (Trench warfare itself had been pioneered fifty years earlier at Spotsylvania during the American Civil War, on the remarkable occasion when two great generals first confronted each other—Grant versus Lee, head to head.)

The only way to *advance* against machine guns was in tanks. Several brilliant Englishmen played central roles in the invention of the tank, most notably Winston Churchill. Being a genius, Churchill naturally altered more than one field forever.

No-man's-land was the space between the trenches. European (and toward the end, American) soldiers repeatedly charged through no-man's-land, where no man belonged or could live. A German observer wrote about the Somme:

> The noise of battle became indescribable. The shouting of orders and the shrill British cheers as they charged forward could be heard above the violent and intense fusillade of machine guns and rifles and bursting bombs, and above the deep thunderings of the artillery and shell explosions. With all this were mingled the moans and

groans of the wounded, the cries for help and the last screams of death. Again and again the extended lines of British infantry broke against the German defense like waves against a cliff, only to be beaten back.

People remember the savage, pointless slaughter if they remember anything about World War I. But there is another aspect of the war that we have forgotten. Virtually the whole world has forgotten it—but it too is important and must be grappled with.

The brilliant left-wing author Mary McCarthy wrote about a Great War veteran in her famous story "The Man in the Brooks Brothers Suit." It was fiction but just barely, according to the author herself; her veteran was based closely on a real person. "I was in the last war," says the hero, speaking of the First World War, "and I had a grand time . . . I haven't had such a good time since the war."

You heard right. It was possible for a soldier of the Great War *to enjoy it.*

Ludwig Wittgenstein was no fiction: he was one of the greatest philosophers of the last hundred years, scion of one of the most distinguished and wealthiest Jewish families in Europe. He was a war hero in the Austro-Hungarian army during World War I. In 1936 he said to a friend and disciple, "Nowadays it is the fashion to emphasize the horrors of the last war. I didn't find it so horrible." This was a profoundly thoughtful man—admittedly, one who enjoyed challenging universal assumptions. "The man was lit up with memories of the war," says McCarthy's (just barely) fictional narrator, "droll stories of horseplay and drinking parties." "It had been, she [the story's narrator] could see, an extension of college days, a sort of

lower-middle-class Grand Tour, a wonderful male roughhouse
that had left a man such as this with a permanent homesickness for fraternity that no stag party could quite ease."

A wonderful male roughhouse? Yes, veterans actually said
such things about the Great War, and we owe it to them to listen carefully and try to understand. American attitudes to war
and danger, bravery and chivalry, are vital to Americanism and
America's national character. Insofar as other nations share aspects of America's character, we must know that also.

★ ★ ★

Of course it is not that Europeans hated the Great War while
Americans lived it up. American soldiers suffered and died
too; they were tremendously brave and inexperienced, Germans said at the time, and that was why they died in such huge
numbers.

And yet it *was* possible for a soldier of the Great War to enjoy it. Such "enjoyment" is not the type you might get out of
(say) a pleasant evening with friends. It is a strange kind of enjoyment, maybe abnormal, even pathological, but real. Robert
E. Lee said it best, after his victory at Fredericksburg: "It is well
that war is so terrible, or we should grow too fond of it."

"In a world from which physical danger has been elimi-
nated," George Orwell wrote in *The Road to Wigan Pier*
(1937), ". . . would physical courage be likely to survive? *Could*
it survive? . . . As for such qualities as loyalty, generosity, etc., in
a world where nothing went wrong, they would not only be ir-
relevant but probably unimaginable. The truth is that many of
the qualities we admire in human beings can only function in
opposition to some kind of disaster, pain or difficulty."

As the war continued, Russia started to fall apart. In March of 1917 the czar (a weak, foolish, miserable autocrat) abdicated, and a liberal, democratic government took power. The new government announced that Russia would continue to fight alongside her allies. But the Russians were tired of fighting and *very* tired of losing—although Russia had fought well in the campaign of 1916. In November 1917 came the Bolshevik Revolution, and Russia's new communist rulers announced that she was getting out—in effect, surrendering to Germany. Germany imposed on Russia the Treaty of Brest-Litovsk, which stripped the Russian Empire of Poland, the Ukraine, Finland, Latvia, Estonia, and Lithuania—it came close, in fact, to creating the map of eastern Europe as it exists today.

With Russia out, Germany rushed her troops from the Eastern Front, where they were no longer needed, to the Western, where they were needed desperately to fight the Allies.

What would happen first? Would Germany crush the Allies, or would American soldiers reach France soon enough and in strength enough to save the West?

America got there in time.

Germany and her allies surrendered. Fighting ended at eleven A.M. on November 11, 1918. The German army turned around and marched sullenly home.

Back in January 1918 Wilson had proposed "Fourteen Points" as a basis for peace: freedom of the seas in peace and war, no more secret treaties, removal of barriers to international trade, armament reductions all around, the evacuation of all occupied territories, national self-determination and a redrawn map of Europe to go along with it, and an international organization to prevent war.

France and Britain had reservations but accepted Wilson's

points by and large. Germany asked for an armistice, under the impression that the Fourteen Points would be the basis of any peace settlement. Things worked out differently.

The Paris Peace Conference convened in January 1919. All serious negotiations were conducted by the "big four"—Wilson, David Lloyd George for Britain, Georges Clemenceau for France, and Vittorio Orlando for Italy. Russia was busy with her red-versus-white civil war; Germany was not invited.

The treaty that finally emerged bore little resemblance to the sort of document the Fourteen Points foreshadowed. In some ways it was harsh: the Germans were ordered to pay reparations equaling the whole cost of the war, amount unspecified. Germany was required to sign a blank check. The famous "war guilt clause" compelled Germany to accept responsibility for imposing war on the Allies. In reality the fault was not wholly Germany's, but the decisive act that had caused Britain to jump in and turn a European fight into a world war was in fact Germany's premeditated, cold-blooded invasion of Belgium. It has often been condemned, but the war guilt clause was not far wrong.

★   ★   ★

Scholarly analysis of World War I began as soon as the fighting ended, sometimes sooner. The scholars' conclusions were the bitterest conceivable news for Europeans. Europe never has got over the First World War and probably never will.

Austria-Hungary did not have to declare war against Serbia on July 28, 1914, but she was in a hurry to forestall proposed negotiations. Russia did not have to mobilize on July 30; she was under no military threat; but she mobilized anyway. Germany did not have to go crashing into Belgium on August 4— she was in no danger of being overrun by hot-headed Flemings—but once she had mobilized on the Belgian border (and she *had* to mobilize because Russia had), her famous Schlieffen plan would be exposed and thereby rendered as useless as light-struck film unless she hit right away.

Looking back, Europe—especially Britain—felt deep remorse. Many Englishmen were convinced that, had Germany *only known for sure* that invading Belgium would bring Britain into the war, the invasion would not have happened. Germany disdained France but respected Britain—envied but did not want to fight her. Many Englishmen felt closer to Germans than to Frenchmen; *France* was England's traditional enemy.

And Britain blamed herself, hard, for having rejoiced at the outbreak of war. She had greeted it with jubilation. All Europe had. "Europeans of all stripes," writes the historian Peter Gay, "joined in greeting war with a fervor bordering on a religious experience." All sorts of Europeans looked forward to a short, dashing war. When the terrible reality dawned and the casualty lists started to roll in, many Europeans felt unbearable grief and guilt—*personal* guilt in proportion to the joy they had expressed when war began. Britain, then and now, had the best-developed conscience in Europe. Several European nations felt guilty, but a huge literature (by historians and memoirists) on Britain, pacifism, and appeasement in the 1920s and 1930s makes clear that Britain felt guiltiest.

Americans had no such crisis of conscience—a hugely important fact that continues to shape world politics to this very day. Americans had done nothing (on purpose or otherwise) to cause the war, and they had not rejoiced when it started. They helped the Allies win and then, for the most part, did their best to forget all about it.

Most Americans today remember the Great War only because they know there was a World War II, so it's fairly clear

there must have been a I. When will the last American veteran
of the Great War die? A few survive, but not many, and they
haven't been paid much attention for a long time. Americans by
and large don't waste time thinking about the First World War.
They know little and care less.

And yet there's a remarkable fact about the world we inhabit
today. *The end of the Cold War and the disintegration of the
Soviet Union were actually the long-delayed end of the Second
World War,* the rusty iron framework collapsing into scrap and
dust at long last. And when the Cold War ended and World War
II disappeared, *finally* . . . the Great War reasserted its powerful
presence in world culture.

Think of it this way: World War II was only the semifinals
in a long match for world domination. In the semifinals the
United States played Imperial Japan; the Soviets played Nazi
Germany. In the finals (aka the Cold War), the United States
beat the Soviets. This view of world history sounds flip, but it
conveys important truth. The Allies made enormous and costly
contributions to beat the Nazis, but the Soviet Union played the
largest role and bore the brunt of the fighting and suffering.
Britain was already finished as a world power when she entered
the Second World War, although her act had another decade or
so to run. Imperial Japan and Nazi Germany represented not so
much allies as parallel attempts to dominate separate parts of
the globe. Victory in World War II transformed the USSR from
an ex-empire staggering from self-inflicted wounds to a superpower with only one serious rival on earth.

It follows that the Cold War was a continuation of the worldwide struggle that began in the 1930s, when Japan and Germany both launched fiercely destructive wars of aggression.
The Cold War's end meant that a fifty-year war (longer if we

start counting in 1931, when Japan invaded China) had finally run its course. When that Fifty Years War was over at last, the Great War reappeared like a mountain long hidden by fog. The world we live in today was shaped not by World War II but by the First World War, which dominates the landscape once again (a commanding, brooding presence) as it did in the 1920s.

Woodrow Wilson, Americanism, and Anti-Americanism

No president spoke the language of Bible, divine mission, and American Zionism more consistently than Woodrow Wilson. And Wilson's speeches make it clear that Americanism inspired his agonized, epochal decision to take America into the war.

His first inaugural address in 1913 is composed in pure and perfect Lincoln-inspired Americanese:

> The feelings with which we face this new age of right and opportunity sweep across our heartstrings like some air out of God's own presence, where justice and mercy are reconciled and the judge and the brother are one.

In time he came to believe that America, grown to be a great power, must fight to bring Americanism to the world. More precisely, he felt that America, if forced to fight for her interests, *must fight for her principles too*. That is Wilsonian, activist Americanism.

Wilson was no lover of military adventures. Like Lincoln, he loved peace. "There is such a thing as a man being too proud to fight," said Wilson, explaining his early reluctance to take America into the war. "There is such a thing as a nation being so right that it does not need to convince others by force that it is right."

The phrase "so right that . . . ," as if rightness had gradations and *American* rightness was the best kind, was typical Wilson. He won reelection in 1916 as the president who had "kept us out of war."

But he changed his mind. Germany's unrestricted submarine warfare was the immediate provocation. Germany knew that, by declaring her readiness to sink American ships, she would bring the United States into the war. She knew but no longer cared. In 1917 the Germans underestimated America; in 1941 they did it again. The Soviets underestimated America at the start of the Cold War in 1947. Saddam Hussein did it in 1990 when he invaded Kuwait, and he did it again in 2003. Terrorists in Iraq are doing it yet again—we hope. But we know all too well that the United States faces two possibilities. She can soldier on and win, as she usually has. Or she can revisit Vietnam and run away.

Wilson insisted that America must fight for her interests *and* her principles. In his April 1917 speech asking for a declaration of war, he told Congress, "The world must be made safe for democracy"—a much-ridiculed phrase, especially in Europe. But that sentence perfectly captures the idea of Americanism as a world religion and the chivalrous responsibility that fell to the citizens of the American Zion. God had blessed them beyond their deserts. They had to acknowledge the gift and spread the blessing.

Wilson defined Americanism in religious terms that implied not just global preaching but global acting: "The right is more precious than peace." That sounds like Lincoln and the Hebrew Bible, and a basic principle of the Old Testament Christianity that has always appealed to Americans.

In urging activist Americanism on the country, Wilson's beliefs rested foursquare on Christianity. His speech to Congress on the declaration of war was intended for Germans as well as Ameri-

cans. He concluded his discussion of American plans with these words: "God helping her, she can do no other." In his classic 1935 history Mark Sullivan drew attention to Wilson's "magnificent combination of subtlety and audacity": "Probably not one in a hundred of his American hearers," Sullivan wrote, "recognized that paraphrase of Martin Luther's declaration, immortal to every German Lutheran, 'Ich kann nicht anders' (I can do no other)."*
In launching an ambitious new interpretation of Americanism, Wilson reached back to the dawn of Protestant Christianity.

He hoped to add to Americanism the idea of global responsibility. He succeeded, at least so far as public opinion *during* the war was concerned.

In a speech after the war defending the peace treaty, he explained that "America may be said to have just reached her majority as a world power." Twenty-one years before, the United States had triumphed in her war against Spain. In the aftermath she became colonial master of the Philippines and established herself as a world power (or an almost world power). "The stage is set, the destiny disclosed," said Wilson at the end of this speech.

It has come about by no plan of our conceiving, but by the hand of God who led us into this way. We cannot turn back. We can only go forward, with lifted eyes and freshened spirit, to follow the vision. It was of this that we dreamed at our birth. America shall in truth show the way. The light streams upon the path ahead, and nowhere else.

*Mark Sullivan, *Our Times, 1900–1925* (New York: Charles Scribner's Sons, 1935), vol. 5, p. 285.

No plainer distillation of American Zionism exists. *It has come about by no plan of our conceiving, but by the hand of God who led us into this way* . . . God led us forward to the promised land and continues to lead us forward. *We can only go forward, with lifted eyes and freshened spirit, to follow the vision* . . . God's vision is the one we are following—which we are privileged and *required* to do because God has chosen us and we must choose God. *America shall in truth show the way.*

★ ★ ★

In studying Wilson, we don't study Americanism alone. We study anti-Americanism too.

Wilson was widely disliked, for many reasons. Some were strictly personal; others cut to the essence of Americanism and American character. Wilson was frankly Christian—he saw his mission as divinely inspired and saw Americans as God's new chosen people with a *duty* to lead. These ideas drove certain people crazy—Europeans especially. Wilson propounded them in a humorless, self-absorbed way. But some thinkers make too much of Wilson's unlovable character. Generations earlier many Britons had been prepared to denounce Lincoln just as bitterly. One large part of Wilson-hatred was plain old America-hatred. And a large part of *that* was dislike of Americanism, of American Christianity, and increasingly of Judeo-Christian religion in general. And some of Wilson's critics made a point of singling out the Old Testament component of Wilson's beliefs as especially obnoxious.

He sailed the Atlantic to attend the Paris peace talks in person. His behavior in Europe—he came, went home to America, and returned for another round—was widely regarded as pompous, officious, cold, and uncomfortably majestic, even by America's friends.

But Wilson made a perfect target (*so* easy to hit!) not only for rational dislike but for irrational contempt. Indeed, much of the British elite grew to loathe him so intensely that he became a political emetic. British intellectuals lost all control and spewed up all sorts of poisonous hatred that they harbored inwardly for the upstart, nouveau-riche, nouveau-powerful nation personified by President Wilson, that preachy, naïve, absurdly religious, childishly idealistic vulgarian. Anti-Americanism became especially acute now that the United States had stepped in and saved Europe's hash.

The celebrated English economist John Maynard Keynes wrote about Wilson that "the defects . . . of his temperament and of his equipment, were fatally apparent."* It was a legitimate ad hominem attack—nasty, of course, but Keynes *was* nasty. But Keynes also wrote, regarding Wilson at the Paris peace talks, "Now it was that what I have called his theological or Presbyterian temperament became dangerous." Educated Englishmen thought Americans were overly prone to Presbyterian (neo-Puritan) thinking.

Eventually Wilson's Fourteen Points became, Keynes wrote, "a document for gloss and interpretation and for all the intellectual apparatus of self-deception, by which, I daresay, the President's forefathers had persuaded themselves that the course they thought it necessary to take was consistent with every syllable of the Pentateuch." This revealing comment shows that, in refined British eyes, America was guilty of childish infatuation not only with the Bible but *especially* with the Old Testament (which begins with the Pentateuch). Later Keynes referred to "the disintegration of the President's moral position and the clouding of his

*John Maynard Keynes, *The Economic Consequences of the Peace* (New York: Harcourt, Brace and Howe, 1920), pp. 49ff.

mind" as "a long theological struggle." Again, it is their theological propensities that make Americans *especially* objectionable.

The British author and diplomat Harold Nicolson agreed.
He called Wilson "the descendant of Covenanters, the inheri-
tor of a more immediate Presbyterian tradition. That spiritual
arrogance which seems inseparable from the harder forms of
religion had eaten deep into his soul."*

The descendant of Covenanters. The harder forms of religion.
America was the Puritan nation. When the President preached
global, activist Americanism, the British saw straight through
to its Puritan origins. Woodrow Wilson had always been transparent.

Epilogue: The Great War and the Modern World

World War I created the environment in which Americanism
exists *today*. When the killing tide subsided, it left pacifism and
appeasement behind like bloody foam on the beach. After and
because of World War I, many Europeans knew in their guts
that (1) war was unthinkably awful, (2) pacifism was mandatory, (3) nationalism (even *nationality*) was dangerous, and (4)
UN-type organizations like the League of Nations were mankind's only hope. These beliefs were temporarily suspended
during World War II, because they were no help in fighting the
Nazis. But they carried so much weight that they induced western Europe to put off challenging Hitler until it was almost too
late. When Britain and France did at last declare war on Nazi
Germany, they entered the fight pitifully outgunned and out-

---

*Sir Harold George Nicolson, *Peacemaking, 1919* (London: Constable and
Co., 1933), p. 198.

manned—because of those same beliefs, because they had come to believe not that "right makes might" (Lincoln's idea) but that *might* is intrinsically *wrong*.

The United States rejected all four European beliefs. The United States herself was not much good against Nazi Germany during the 1930s—but that was the result of lazy isolationism, not pacifism.

World War I left behind a tripartite world in which three clashing plates define the tectonics of modern society, creating conflict and misery wherever they smash up against each other: Americanism in the middle, with (roughly speaking) power-haters on one side and power-lovers on the other. All three schools existed before the First World War, but the Great War set them up in modern form and threw the switch that jolted these huge plates into rumbling, jarring, killing motion.

Furthermore, *Europe today is essentially the Europe that emerged from the First World War.* The landscapes of the Second World War and the Cold War have nearly vanished. The emerging post–Cold War "new world order" of 1990s and 2000s Europe is oddly familiar. It's amazingly like the Europe of the 1920s, with its love of self-determination and its loathing of imperialism and war; its liberal Germany and its weak, shrunken, uneasy Russia (a shadow of its former imperial self); its map crammed with small states; its casual, endemic anti-Semitism; its politically, financially, and masochistically rewarding fascination with Muslim states that despise it; its undertone of self-hatred and guilt; and, of course, its contempt for America.

We need to understand these things about Europe (Europe's influence extends worldwide) in order to understand what Americanism means today, and what Americanism is up against.

Today all Europe seems convinced, just as Britain was in the

1920s and 1930s, that war must never happen again. In the mid-1930s British prime minister Stanley Baldwin was said to be "for peace at any price." In 1938 the politician Thomas Jones, Baldwin's close friend, wrote that "we have to convince the world that for peace we are prepared to go to absurd lengths." That's what appeasement was and *is* like.

Back in the 1920s *appeasement* was born as a modern movement—the idea that instead of challenging and beating your enemies you should placate them, *make* them your friends. Today appeasement rules Europe once again. The European mainstream believes passionately in appeasement—and disdains the American mainstream for passionately, contemptuously *rejecting* appeasement.

During World War I western Europe experienced the psychological devastation of a bloodbath, of sheer hideous, pointless slaughter. Naturally many Europeans became supporters of appeasement. ("Resist not evil.") America had been spared the experience, and naturally *rejected* appeasement. ("The Lord will grant strength to His people; the Lord will bless His people with peace.") But eventually American *intellectuals* had the same nightmare experience that western Europe had lived through. Unlike Americans at large, intellectuals saw the Vietnam War as *exactly* sheer hideous, pointless slaughter, as America's First World War. While most Americans continued to believe in peace through strength, American intellectuals (spooked by Vietnam) came to believe in appeasement. The Vietnam War had been fought largely by the working classes. But you cannot believe seriously in appeasement unless you feel guilty.

The history of modern American culture is encapsulated in these grimly simple facts.

CHAPTER 7

THE EMERGENCE OF
MODERN AMERICANISM

The threats posed by World War II and the Cold War were two large challenges to the Wilsonian vision of activist Americanism. Wilson had argued that American true believers were responsible to all mankind and that they had to act on American Zionism by spreading the Creed all over the world.

But Franklin Roosevelt did *not* take America into the Second World War. By helping Britain against Germany and China against Japan, he went right to the brink but did not cross over it. (He was a master of the near thing, an artist at precise political calculation.) America fought in the Second World War because Tokyo and then Berlin (and Rome) declared war on the United States. We didn't enlist; we were drafted.

Harry Truman handled things differently. He believed in activist Americanism. He accepted the Soviet challenge and took the United States into the Cold War. It's possible that Roosevelt would have done the same; it's much easier to enter a cold war than a hot one. But it's not surprising that Truman acted as he did. Like Wilson, Truman was profoundly attached both to the Bible and to the biblical religion called Americanism. Truman and Wilson had both been reared in homes full of the Bible and Protestant Christianity.*

The Cold War into which Truman boldly led America continued until Ronald Reagan advanced a novel idea: why not win it? As president, he led America to the brink of victory—and only a year after Reagan was succeeded by the first George Bush, victory followed. If Bill Clinton's legacy shortly after leaving office was 9/11, Reagan's was the collapse of the Soviet Empire. It may be that Americanism was *the* strongest influence in Reagan's spiritual life, even stronger than Christianity.

The Cold War ended with the collapse of the Soviet Union in 1990. In the aftermath America faced the same problem that Truman had faced in the late 1940s. Was Americanism an active or a passive faith? Were we obliged to spread the Creed or only preach it? George W. Bush lined up with Truman and Wilson and arguably the spirit of Lincoln. Of course the nation must defend itself, but Bush has insisted that spreading the Creed is good for mankind *and* America. Like Wilson and Truman, he is a decidedly Christian president, who opens every cabinet meeting with a prayer.

This chapter is arranged differently from earlier ones, be-

---

*Roosevelt is assumed to have been distinctly less attached to the Bible and religion than Wilson and Truman were. But a new anthology of passages from Roosevelt's presidential papers makes it seem possible that historians have underestimated the seriousness of Roosevelt's Christianity. See William J. Federer, *The Faith of FDR: From President Franklin Delano Roosevelt's Public Papers, 1933–1945* (St. Louis: Amerisearch, 2006).

cause it has several focuses. Its five sections are ordered chronologically: World War II and Franklin Roosevelt; Truman and the start of the Cold War; the 1960s and the opening of the culture war that is still under way; Reagan and the winning of the Cold War; and finally, the state of affairs today.

The Second World War

From the standpoint of American foreign policy, the three most important U.S. presidents of the twentieth century were Woodrow Wilson, Harry Truman, and Ronald Reagan.

It may seem bizarre to omit Franklin Roosevelt. Roosevelt defended America heroically: he kept up the nation's morale during the Great Depression of the 1930s—and transformed the American government into the enormous bureaucracy it is today, growing constantly like a coral reef at a million points simultaneously. Without FDR, an antidemocratic insurgency might have overturned Americanism in this country during the worst days of the Depression. It was unlikely, but possible. Would a nation that survived the Civil War have succumbed to an economic depression? But *would* it have survived the Civil War without Lincoln's leadership? And might not FDR have been equally crucial during the Depression?

Evaluating Roosevelt fairly, however, requires confronting the fact that America entered the Second World War because it was pushed. Japan attacked Pearl Harbor; then Hitler declared war on America, and Mussolini followed. By contrast, Woodrow Wilson *decided* that America must enter World War I. Harry Truman *decided* that America must enter the Cold War. Ronald Reagan *decided* that America must win the Cold War. But FDR *did not decide* that America must enter World War II. That decision was made for us, in Tokyo and Berlin. It was made in Rome too, but Mussolini wasn't much of an adversary compared with the Nazis and the Japanese.

Britain, on the other hand, entered World War II on purpose, for the same reason she had entered World War I: to protect a small state that had been invaded by Germany. In 1939 as in 1914, she had not been attacked. In fact, Hitler had repeatedly signaled his wish to live at peace with the British Empire, which he grudgingly admired. (America he despised.) Britain declared war because Germany had attacked Poland; Britain had promised to defend Poland. (Recall that Britain had a long-standing policy of preventing any one power from dominating the European Continent.)

But Roosevelt took America to war only when he had no choice. True, he went far beyond neutrality to help Britain during 1940 and 1941, before Pearl Harbor. Britain might not have survived those years without American aid, including naval support against U-boats in the western Atlantic. American aid against Japan was also substantial well before Pearl Harbor and was regarded by Japan as highly provocative.

Yet America might *never* have got into World War II had she not been attacked. And this observation must be evaluated against the abnormal state of U.S. public opinion after the fall of France in June 1940; it was stunned into fluidity. Anything might have happened. The fall of France was an astonishing bolt from the blue. FDR was a brilliant persuader and a much-admired leader. In June 1940 he could probably have talked Congress and America into declaring war on Hitler *if he had wanted to*. But we'll never know for sure, because he did not want to; or at least he never tried to.

But Japan made the decision, and shortly after Pearl Harbor World War II became the biggest war in history, with Britain and America fighting Germany and Japan, Soviet Russia fighting Germany, China fighting Japan, and many other combatants—from Australia and the Dutch East Indies to Canada, to Greece, and many more. For our part we are left with nothing less than the deepest unanswered question in modern history. The following paragraphs are only a brief outline of the question; they are no answer.

Americanism is a biblical religion. So are Judaism and Christianity. World War II poses questions about all biblical religions in the largest sense. But they might not be the questions you anticipate.

The deepest unanswered question in modern history is also the deepest *unasked* one. We are a secular civilization, with a highly secular intelligentsia. We don't like pondering religion.

To understand this vast, deep question, we must start by considering a basic fact about the Second World War. It was a period of unspeakable evil. Morality collapsed and was trampled to death in three of the world's largest nations simultaneously.

And the question is this: What does it mean—what *could* it mean—that *each one* of the three worst criminal states, Nazi Germany, Stalinist Russia, and Imperial Japan, had recently gone over to a national system of state paganism? (Those systems were Führer-worship and the "Führer principle" in Germany, Stalin-worship in the Soviet Union, and a newly aggressive and militaristic form of Shinto and emperor-worship in Japan.) And what does it mean that the two states that led the crusade to annihilate tyranny and reestablish decency—Britain and later the United States—both called themselves, informally, *Christian states?*

These questions need amplification. Hitler's barbarism is

well known, but Stalin's was just as bestial. Between fifteen and
thirty million people died in the prisons and labor camps of the
Soviet gulag.* Imperial Japan was just as evil in its brutality to
Allied POWs and captive Asian peoples.

Most westerners understand that Nazi Germany and Stalinist Russia are textbook examples of state paganism; wartime
Japan is less well understood. In the 1920s a code of knightly
conduct called *bushido* was reintroduced in a newly militarized
form. Shinto was transformed from an ancient minority religion into a warlike cult devoted to the militaristic, totalitarian
regime. Emperor-worship became a national practice, especially prominent in the military.

Three grotesquely evil states; three pagan regimes.

A pair of strange anomalies underline the enormous unanswered question: the anomaly of a "good state" in the Axis and
the evil state among the Allies. Fascist Italy was Germany's friend.
At Hitler's urging, Mussolini decreed anti-Semitism in fascist
Italy. Italy was a ruthlessly ambitious, if not terribly effective, ag-
gressor before and during World War II, until its surrender to the
Allies and its partial occupation by Germany in 1943. Yet Italy
was incapable of inflicting Nazi-style barbarism on its Jewish population or on captive peoples in conquered nations. And Italy—
unlike Germany, unlike Japan—never went over to state

---

*The historian Robert Conquest gives some facts. A prisoner at Kholod-
naya Gora had to stuff his ears with bread before sleeping on account of the
shrieks of women being interrogated nearby. At the Kolyma in Siberia, inmates labored twelve-hour days in frozen gold mines. Work outside was
compulsory until temperatures reached -50°C. Fur clothing was banned;
later, felt shoes were replaced by canvas. Living at fifty below in cheap
sneakers, on almost no food, doing backbreaking labor: at one camp 1,300 of
3,000 inmates died in one year.

paganism; Italy considered herself a Christian nation throughout the fascist years.

Great Britain and the U.S. called themselves Christian countries. But their cobelligerent Soviet Russia was a pagan nation with a leader cult strongly resembling Germany's—and the USSR practiced evil on the same scale as its enemy Nazi Germany. Stalin was the only world leader whom Hitler admired. (But in the closing months of the war Germans did anything whatsoever to get *out* of places the Soviets were going to capture and *into* ones that would be occupied by America or Britain or France.)

There is no neat or simple pattern here. France considered herself a Christian nation during the war but took almost as much satisfaction as Germany in persecuting Jews. Austria under the Nazis was generally more "Christian" than Germany, but it was at least as barbarous. Most Poles were devout Catholics—and some were also enthusiastic Nazi collaborators when it came to murdering Jews. Christianity per se does not emerge (not hardly!) covered with glory.

And yet. In those terrible years when civilization collapsed into barbarism in three of the world's leading nations ... the leading barbarians and their followers were pagans who reveled in their paganism. And the two nonbarbarian nations that led the fight against barbarism were Christian nations. And their armies consisted largely of Christians—and a few Jews.*

Of course the Chinese and many Indians, Burmese, Filipinos, and other Asian peoples fought too. Most were not Christian.

But is it possible that, when the chips were down, in the most

---

*Although there were disproportionately many Jews in the American armed forces relative to the number of Jews in the population. The same pattern held during World War I and the Civil War.

terrible crisis civilization had ever seen, Christianity *did indeed* help save the world? Can we avoid classifying state paganism as an inducement to evil, and Christianity—especially but not exclusively Protestant, biblical Christianity—as an inducement to good? Can we avoid suspecting that a nation's religious life might indeed be important in a crisis? Can we avoid suspecting that religion will save a nation's soul if anything can?

These questions are rarely asked. Most historians, philosophers, and even theologians don't seem interested. But every citizen of the world has a duty to ponder them. The answers are obviously important to any serious evaluation of Americanism, America's moral character, and the role of religion in American life.

Truman's Americanism

When Roosevelt died in April 1945, Harry Truman took over as leader of America, the United Nations alliance, and the free world—and presided over the end of World War II and the start of the Cold War.

Truman was born in Lamar, Missouri, in May 1884. His mother enrolled him in a Presbyterian Sunday school because it was "the nearest Protestant Church." Later in life he sometimes attended Baptist churches. He wrote in his memoirs, "By the time I was thirteen or fourteen," he had read "our big old Bible three times through." He studied the Bible his whole life; he read it through another seven times during his White House years alone. As a young man he was fascinated by history—which "revealed to me," he wrote, "that what came about in Philadelphia in 1776 really had its beginning in Hebrew times." This thought harmonizes perfectly with American Zionism.

Americanism and patriotism were important to Truman his

whole life long. But I will focus here on Truman's Americanism during his almost two terms in the White House. He took over at Roosevelt's death, near the start of FDR's fourth term, was elected in his own right in 1948, then retired to become a senior eminence.

When Truman became president in April 1945, World War II was still under way and Soviet Russia was America's more-or-less-trusted ally. Roosevelt had been reluctant to heed Churchill's increasingly pointed warnings about Stalin. To Churchill it was becoming plainer by the minute that Stalin would be a dangerous handful after the war, with much of eastern and central Europe in the bloody claws of his gigantic, voracious Red Army—which was well trained and kept on a short leash.

Truman tells us that the early days of his presidency were full of religious thoughts. (The fighting with Germany was nearly finished, but the war with Japan was far from over.) If hard times reveal what a man is made of, then we know what Truman was all about. After his first trip as president to the Capitol, he was greeted by page boys and reporters. "Boys, if you ever pray, pray for me now," he told them. "As I went to bed that night," he wrote, "I prayed that I would be equal to the task." His first speech to Congress concluded,

> I humbly pray God in the words of King Solomon, "Give therefore Thy servant an understanding heart to judge Thy people, that I may discern good and bad: for who is able to judge this Thy so great a people?" I ask only to be a good and faithful servant of my Lord and my people.

A perfect expression of Christianity first, then Americanism; naturally Truman identified himself with the ruler of the Is-

raelite nation and "Thy people" with the *American* people—
like a true believer in American Zionism.

Soon after that first congressional address, he spoke by radio to
American armed forces around the world. He finished by quoting
Lincoln: "With malice toward none; with charity for all; with
firmness in the right, as God gives us to see the right, let us strive
on to finish the work we are in." Later that month he spoke by radio to delegates in San Francisco for the first meeting of the
United Nations organizing conference. "As we are about to under-
take our heavy duties," he began, "we beseech Almighty God to
guide us in building a permanent monument to those who gave
their lives that this moment might come." (He echoed Lincoln:
for those who here gave their lives that that nation might live.)
"May He lead our steps in His own righteous path of peace." (He
echoed the Bible: *Her ways are ways of pleasantness, and all her
paths are peace.* Prov. 3:17, regarding the Lord's Torah.)

It was customary for presidents to talk religion on public occasions. But Truman went far beyond minimal requirements,
and his sincerity is plain.

In March 1947 he announced the Truman Doctrine. Greece
and Turkey were facing Soviet-backed communist insurgen-
cies. Britain had been supporting the hard-pressed Greek and
Turkish governments but couldn't afford to continue. Truman
pressed Congress to take over from the British and provide finan-
cial and military aid to Greece and Turkey. And he proclaimed
that America must support free peoples all over the world.

His presidency was full of big events, but this one shaped
American foreign policy for the next forty years. The Truman
Doctrine took America into the Cold War. Truman's decision to
accept the Soviet challenge reflected Churchill's ripening ideas.

(Churchill was no longer prime minister, but in 1946 he had delivered the famous speech in which he spoke of the "iron curtain" that had fallen across much of central and eastern Europe.) Truman's epochal decision also reflected the president's devout Americanism.

So America would oppose the expansion of communism and help spread the American way. "Our way of life is based upon the will of the majority," said Truman, "and is distinguished by free institutions, representative government, free elections, guarantees of individual liberty, freedom of speech and religion and freedom from political oppression." It was Truman's own version of the Creed. No one ever called him eloquent; Lincoln's soaring poetry was beyond him. But his homely, meat-loaf prose (nothing fancy, nothing phony) had its own appeal, and still does.

"The free peoples of the world," said Truman, "look to us for support in maintaining their freedoms." *I believe in America:* lots of people were saying so that very moment. Truman knew it.

He did not and could not propose that America rush to the aid of *all* threatened and oppressed peoples, but at least it could rush to the aid of *some.* He wrote later, "This was, I believe, a turning point in America's foreign policy." It was a turning point that FDR had never envisioned. The United States had helped rescue millions of people during the Second World War, but America entered the Cold War voluntarily.

Truman's own subsequent speeches about the new doctrine tell us what he had in mind, what moved and motivated the new policy. "We have a heritage that constitutes the greatest resource of this nation," he said in his single most revealing pronouncement. "I call it the spirit and character of the American people." Others called it Americanism pure and simple.

Truman reached many immensely important foreign policy decisions. He gave Marshall Plan aid to Europe. He led America and the United Nations into the Korean War, and then he refused to allow General Douglas MacArthur—who commanded American troops in Korea and had his own ideas about fighting communism—to dictate Korean policy. Few presidential terms in office have been more eventful.

The American Religion was central to one other highly important Truman foreign policy decision. In 1948 Truman overruled many of his own advisers and made the United States the first nation in the world to recognize the just-created, newly proclaimed State of Israel. That act brought the story of Americanism full circle. The first Puritan settlers in the New World were inspired by an ancient Jewish state that had disappeared two thousand years ago.

America and Israel are tied together by more than politics and sentiment. Each resembles the other more than any other nation on earth. Each was created by persecuted ex-Europeans who came to a sparsely settled promised land clutching their Bibles, ready to make the wilderness bloom and to build or rebuild a shining city on a hill, prepared to fight for a place in this world where each one of them could sit "every man under his vine and under his fig tree; and none could make them afraid" (Mic. 4:4).*

---

*The biggest difference between the two might be—ironically—Israel's quasi-socialist economy. Many Israeli settlers arrived with the same bias in favor of communal ownership as certain Puritan settlers in America. But we have no idea what Israel's economy would be like today if she had been allowed to develop normally, without the constant threat and frequent reality of war.

Truman's adviser Clark Clifford commented on his boss:

> From his reading of the Old Testament he felt the Jews derived a legitimate historical right to Palestine, and he sometimes cited such biblical lines as Deuteronomy 1:8: "Behold, I have given up the land before you; go in and take possession of the land which the Lord hath sworn unto your fathers, to Abraham, to Isaac and to Jacob."*

The chief rabbi of the newly created State of Israel told Truman, "God put you in your mother's womb so you would be the instrument to bring the rebirth of Israel after two thousand years." "I thought he was overdoing things," commented Truman's aide David Niles, respecting the rabbi's announcement. "But when I looked over at the President, tears were running down his cheeks." Niles was a Jew who had served on FDR's staff also. Had Roosevelt lived, Niles said later, things might not have turned out nearly so well for the brand-new Jewish state.

After he left office, the Jewish Theological Seminary in Manhattan gave Truman an honorary degree. He was introduced as "the man who helped create the state of Israel," and he began his speech by saying, "Yes, I am Cyrus," the Persian king who had restored the exiled Jews to their homeland roughly twenty-six hundred years earlier. Truman knew the

---

*See Shalom Goldman, *God's Sacred Tongue* (Chapel Hill: University of North Carolina Press, 2004). The historian David McCullough writes, "It was not just American Jews who were stirred by the prospect of a new nation for the Jewish people, it was most Americans." See his *Truman* (New York: Simon & Schuster, 1992), p. 293.

Bible and believed it. Under Truman, America honorably and nobly paid a debt to history.

During the Cold War

In the years after the Truman Doctrine was announced, America invested enormous sums of energy, money, and (sometimes) blood in many countries. By and large, western Europe followed the American or British model of government, and in the late 1940s and 1950s American money and support helped beat off local communist threats to western European nations. But western Europe had long been familiar with democracy. South Korea and South Vietnam are better examples of massive American Cold War investment. In both cases America was satisfied with noncommunist, nontotalitarian governments and did not insist on liberty, democracy, and equality. The United States believed itself to be in no position to push such ambitious programs as the American Creed. Where communism was a threat, preserving a modicum of national independence and personal liberty was the most America could risk—or so it believed. Her main efforts were directed at beating back the communist onslaught.

Japan is a fascinating example of what the United States would like to have done all over the world, an example of spreading the American Creed outside Europe. The internal communist threat was insignificant in Japan during the years when American forces occupied the country following World War II; and the Soviet Union posed no serious external threat. When the waters were safe, America jumped in and spread the Creed. But during the Cold War most waters were dangerous.

Vietnam turned out to be very different from Japan. The war there defined the middle years of the Cold War and helped create a profound change in the U.S. cultural climate that persists to this day. After Vietnam, Americanism was no longer universal within America itself.

To understand the Vietnam War's effect on American culture, remember that Vietnam was America's World War I. American intellectuals responded to the ongoing war by preaching appeasement and pacifism, the doctrine that originated (in modern times) in 1920s England. In consequence, the United States split roughly in half. Conservative Americans still believe in Americanism, by and large, although activist Americanism has always been controversial. (It has always been more popular when an activist foreign policy seems to be working and less popular when it doesn't.) Nowadays American liberals tend not to believe in Americanism—or more precisely, in America. Americanism used to be above politics. There were always disagreements about interpretation, but all religious communities breed such disagreements. For a substantial body of Americans *not to believe* in Americanism, in America's message and mission, is a new thing. The big change was triggered by Vietnam.

Liberal opinion on the Vietnam War is still dominated by four big falsehoods. Those who held these views during the war itself weren't necessarily wrongheaded; in most cases they were telling the truth as they understood it. But today, decades later, it requires an act of will to keep one's ignorance pristine.

Falsehood 1: We were wrong to fight the Vietnamese communists in the first place; they only wanted what was best for their country. In *Why We Were in Vietnam* Norman Podhoretz summarizes Vietnam after the communist victory. He quotes the liberal *New York Times* columnist Tom Wicker, an outspoken critic of the war, on its aftermath: "What Vietnam has given us instead of a

bloodbath [is] a vast tide of human misery in southeast Asia."
He quotes Truong Nhu Tang, minister of justice in the Provi-
sional Revolutionary Government that ruled South Vietnam after Congress ordered the Americans to run away in April, 1975:
"Never has any previous regime brought such masses of people
to such desperation. Not the military dictators, not the colonial-
ists, not even the ancient Chinese overlords." Prominent South
Vietnamese were thrown into prison by the communist regime
and tortured with revoltingly inventive cruelty. Virtually the
whole South Vietnamese army and government were herded
into concentration camps. Tang fled Vietnam in 1979, one of
untold thousands who put to sea in crowded, rickety little boats.
They would do anything to get free of communist Vietnam, the
workers' and peasants' paradise, Fonda-land by the Sea. In Vietnam as everywhere else on earth, *communism* was another word
for death.

Maybe democratic chivalry was not such a bad idea after all.
When we waded into Vietnam to promote our interests *and our
principles*, our mission was to save the people of South Vietnam
from terrorists and tyrants. It was a noble mission.

*Falsehood 2: The Vietnam War was unwinnable. We had no bus-
iness sending our men to a war they were bound to lose.* The
communist Vietcong launched their first major coordinated offensive in January 1968, the "Tet offensive." "Tet was a military disaster for Hanoi," writes the historian Derek Leebaert.
"Intended to destroy South Vietnamese officialdom and spark
a popular uprising, Tet ironically had more of an effect in turning South Vietnam's people against the North." But America
had been fighting ineffectively. In May 1968 Creighton

Abrams replaced William Westmoreland as supreme American commander in Vietnam, and U.S. strategy snapped to, immediately. With Abrams in charge, the war "was being won on the ground," writes the historian Lewis Sorley, "even as it was being lost at the peace table and in the U.S. Congress." The British counterinsurgency expert Sir Robert Thompson comments on America's "Christmas bombing" campaign of 1972, which devastated the North: "You had won the war. It was over." American antiwarriors insisted on losing it anyway.

Falsehood 3: As the American people learned the facts, they turned against the war and forced America's withdrawal from Vietnam. Actually Americans continued to support the war nearly until the end. The 1972 presidential election was a referendum on the war. "Come home, America!" said the antiwar Democrat George McGovern—and lost to Richard Nixon in a landslide. Of all U.S. population segments, eighteen-to-twenty-four-year-old men—who were subject to the draft and did the fighting—were consistently the war's strongest supporters. "It was not the American people which lost its stomach," writes the British thinker Paul Johnson; "it was the American leadership."

Falsehood 4: The real heroes of Vietnam were the protesters and draft resisters who forced America to give up a disastrously wrong policy. If this was heroism, I'll take cowardice. While college students paraded and protested and whooped it up, America's working classes bore the brunt of the fighting and dying. Around 80 percent of the 2.5 million enlisted men who fought in Vietnam came from poor or working-class families. They lacked the lawbreaking and draft-evading skills of their

better-educated countrymen. And they lacked the heart to say
no when their country called. Reread Norman Mailer's gor-
geously written yet (like the smell of marijuana) faintly disgusting *Armies of the Night,* about a massive antiwar march on
the Pentagon. You will learn or relearn all about the passionate
ingenuity of left-wing lawyers fighting for clients they admired—who regarded themselves as innately superior to the
law but were scared of the consequences when they broke it.

★   ★   ★

And so the Vietnam Memorial of 1982 resembled Europe's
memorials to the World War I dead. The 58,152 Americans
who died in Vietnam numbered fewer than Britain's casualties
in many a single battle of World War I. Everyone fears war; almost everyone hates it. But America's response to Vietnam was
like an allergic reaction, in which a relatively small exposure
has catastrophic effects. The Vietnam War, like World War I,
seemed to sensitize Western intellectuals to such an extent that
they grew incapable of tolerating war, couldn't bear even the
thought of it—although as I have noted, intellectuals suffered
far less in Vietnam than did other segments of the U.S. population (workers' children, for example), who were able to bear it
a lot better; who showed no "allergic sensitivity" at all.

The Vietnam War was the main event of the Cold War's
middle years. When Vietnam was over and America had with-
drawn in disgrace, the Cold War was still under way. Between
the end of Vietnam (1975) and the election of Ronald Reagan
(1980), no one thought much about *winning* the Cold War—
except Ronald Reagan. *And* a small, brilliant group of former
left-wing intellectuals who had turned conservative—or (maybe)
had stayed behind as their former colleagues marched leftward.
These were the "new" or "neo" conservatives.

Ronald Reagan would face down the Soviet Union. With a mighty shove (or a kick in the pants), he was destined to send the Soviets reeling toward the "ash-heap of history" (in Leon Trotsky's phrase).

But he was acutely aware at the same time that the communists were doomed anyway, in the long run. Many American intellectuals disagreed. They were positive that the Soviets were holding their own or actually beating the West. Professor Seweryn Bialer of Columbia University said in 1982, "The Soviet Union is not now nor will it be during the next decade in the throes of a true system crisis, for it boasts enormous unused reserves of political and social stability that suffice to endure the deepest difficulties." And Professor John Kenneth Galbraith of Harvard said in 1984, "The Russian system succeeds because, in contrast to the Western industrial economies, it makes full use of its manpower."

The point is not to ridicule these mistaken profs and others like them. It is simply to underline the fact that, while some liberals today like to argue that "Reagan made no difference, the Soviet Union was on the way out anyway," they did not necessarily see things that way at the time. But Reagan did.

Ronald Reagan's Americanism

In some ways Ronald Reagan's relationship to religion resembled Teddy Roosevelt's or Churchill's more than Wilson's or Truman's. (Roosevelt and Churchill were Christians without hesitation, but Christianity and the Bible meant relatively little to them.) Reagan was no Bible-quoter, and he sometimes sounded skeptical on the topic of organized religion. But if we take him at his word, his religious feelings were just as deep as

Wilson's; they were merely less biblical and more mystical. And they were biblical too, on occasion.

His ideas about Americanism are easily understood. Starting in the 1950s, he spoke of his belief in America's "divine mission." He believed deeply in Americanism. When he was president, his speeches on the topic were famous for their moving ardor. And he saw the American Religion as Truman and Wilson had: we must *act* on Americanism by spreading the Creed all over the world. Chivalry strongly appealed to him.

Of course, he was a Christian too. In 1974 he wrote, "I've always believed that we were—each of us—put here for a reason, that there is a plan, a divine plan for all of us." Such feelings are easier to sustain if you are a wildly successful public figure, as Reagan had been for a long time. But he seems to have had this belief since childhood. He learned it from his mother.*

The presidency often deepens a man's religious faith. An attempt on a person's life tends to do likewise, and the attempt on Reagan's life in March 1981 deepened his religious faith and his belief in his own and the nation's mission. But shortly *before* the assassination attempt Reagan had made this assertion in a Washington speech: "The Marxist vision of man without God must eventually be seen as an empty and a false faith—the second oldest in the world—first proclaimed in the Garden of Eden with whispered words of temptation: 'Ye shall be as gods.' "

And after the gunshot nearly killed him, he wrote in his diary: "I know it's going to be a long recovery. Whatever happens now I owe my life to God and will try to serve him every way I can."

---

*See Dinesh D'Souza, *Ronald Reagan: How an Ordinary Man Became an Extraordinary Leader* (New York: Free Press, 1997).

His Americanism was devout. He believed deeply in the Creed *and* in American Zionism. He delivered one of his best-remembered speeches at Pointe du Hoc, Normandy, in honor of the D-Day veterans:

> The men of Normandy had faith that what they were doing was right, faith that they fought for all humanity, faith that a just God would grant them mercy on this beachhead or on the next. It was the deep knowledge— and pray God we have not lost it—that there is a profound moral difference between the use of force for liberation and the use of force for conquest.

War, Lincoln knew, could be an instrument of God's justice. *On this beachhead or on the next* was one of the century's best pieces of presidential speechwriting, subtly capturing the Puritan view of heaven as a beach to be stormed by Christian soldiers.

Reagan will be remembered for his resolve to win the Cold War; for leaning hard on the Soviet Union and helping bring about its collapse. He did not leave that collapse to chance. His arms buildup and especially his Strategic Defense Initiative (SDI) were feats that the Soviets could not have duplicated even if they died trying. The launching of the SDI project "was the most effective single act to bring that old *apparatchik* to his senses," said Genrikh Trofimenko, adviser to the Soviet Foreign Ministry, speaking of Gorbachev, last Soviet emperor.

And Reagan furnished his own side with inspiring leadership. In one of his favorite, best-remembered phrases, he told the world that America was and must always be the "shining city upon a hill." "The phrase comes from John Winthrop," he

explained, "who wrote it to describe the America he imag-
ined." Winthrop wrote those words, as I have said, aboard the
Arabella bound for Massachusetts in 1630. Reagan's use of
these words connected late-twentieth-century America to the
humane Christian vision, the Puritan vision, the *biblical* vision
that created this nation.

George W. Bush and the World Today

Are true-believing Americans obliged merely to accept that the
Creed is true for the whole world, or must they try to *make* it
true for the whole world—gradually, prudently, responsibly,
one tyrant at a time? Does American Zionism mean that America must perfect herself as a model, or that America must *act?*
No Wilsonian argues that America should send the marines to
mow down all the world's tyrants double-quick and then come
home; no anti-Wilsonian argues that spreading liberty, equality, and democracy is a bad thing in principle. But an activist is
glad of any prudent opportunity to spread the Creed, including
by force, and an antiactivist is suspicious of any "opportunity"
that leads to foreign entanglements.

The controversy continues, as it has since Wilson's time. Lincoln had said, how can we be contented believers in Americanism if any American is not free? Bush says (building on
Lincoln, Wilson, Truman, and Reagan), how can we be contented believers in Americanism if *anyone* is not free?

Reagan had opened the door, and George W. Bush walked
through. (He resembles Reagan more than he does his father;
George H. W. Bush did not aspire to sweep away tyrants and
spread freedom.) With the end of the Soviet Union, there

remained limitations on America's ability to act. Communist China was the largest, and America was limited in its dealing with any nuclear power. Yet the United States is much freer today than it ever was before to plant Americanism, or try to, all over the globe. Bush does not seek to convert foreign nations to Americanism by force; he seeks to remove tyrants by force and in so doing to allow nations to choose the American Creed if they want to. But he takes for granted that liberty, equality, and democracy are sacred; and that any people with the chance to choose them *will do so.*

Bush seems to have had a fairly wild youth. (He did graduate from Yale, serve as a fighter pilot in the Texas Air National Guard, and pick up a business degree at Harvard; it couldn't have been all *that* wild.) He married Laura Welch in 1977. She was a Methodist. Nine years later he became one too, a Methodist and a born-again Christian. (He had been Episcopalian.) By the late 1980s he was a serious, ambitious young man.

Clearly Bush is willing to rearrange, even revolutionize, his world-outlook on occasion. So far he has done it twice. He stopped drinking and cleaned up his life when he became a born-again Christian. His second big change followed the terrorist attacks of 9/11; by that time he was President of the United States, and the attacks gave his presidency a focus and a cause. Why did he invade Iraq despite widespread opposition abroad and at home? Obviously he believed that Iraq had weapons of mass destruction; so did every other national leader in the free world, and most other American politicians. In the event, the weapons were not there. (Perhaps they had been made to disappear, possibly into Syria.) But Bush had other motives too.

He knew that Saddam Hussein was a vicious tyrant who was torturing his own people to death. He knew that America had the power to take him out. He knew also that the military machine his father had launched against Saddam after the invasion of Kuwait could easily have gone all the way to Baghdad and liberated Iraq, but hadn't. He knew that desperate Chinese students in Tienanmen Square had begged America for help when his father was president—and had gotten none.

Maybe he was haunted by how little America had done for the world in the years following the Soviet collapse. Or maybe he was one of those sons who admire their fathers so much, they want to be just like them only more so. This type of son sometimes looks back at his father's mistakes and says, I see where the problem was; I can fix it. But such mistakes are not always as easily fixed as they seem.

Or maybe George W. Bush simply saw an opportunity to make America safer and to spread the Creed. Of course, he underestimated the degree to which terrorists would attack liberal democracy on principle; terrorists hate the American Creed and hope to destroy it. That was why they attacked America in the first place. And that was why it was inevitable (in hindsight) that they would attack the American Creed as soon as it put down roots in Iraq.

Bush's activism has, predictably, split the ranks of American true believers. The split is felt in practice as a disagreement among American conservatives. Some, who call themselves realists, or conservatives, say the president is acting un-conservatively. Others, sometimes called internationalists or neoconservatives, defend Bush's view.

The realists argue that foreign adventures are justifiable only to the extent they advance American interests at a reasonable cost. Any other goals are inadmissible. This, they add, is the course of "true conservatism."

Defenders of activist Americanism see a basic moral question. American policy must be guided by Lincoln's words: *with firmness in the right as God gives us to see the right.* "The right" changed dramatically when the Cold War ended. America was left with new duties that could not be shrugged off.

What duties? Here is a parable. If you are the biggest boy on the playground and there are no adults around, the playground is your responsibility. It is your duty to prevent outrages— because your moral code demands that outrages be prevented, and for now you are the only one who can prevent them.

If you are one of *two* biggest boys, and the other one orders you not to protect the weak lest he bash you and everyone else he can grab, then your position is more complicated. Your duty depends on the nature of the outrage that ought to be stopped, and on other circumstances. That was America's position during the Cold War: our moral obligation to overthrow tyrants was limited by the Soviet threat of war.

But today things are different. We are the one and only biggest boy. If there is to be justice in the world, America must create it. No one else will act if the biggest boy won't. Some Americans turn to the United Nations the way they wish they could turn to their mothers. It's not easy to say, "The responsibility is mine and I must wield it." But that's what the United States must say. No UN agency or fairy godmother will bail us out.

Of course, America's moral duty remains complicated. We must pursue justice, help the suffering, and overthrow tyrants. We must spread the Creed. But there are limits to our power. We must pick our tyrants carefully, keeping in mind not only justice but our practical interests and the worldwide consequences of what we intend. Our duty to spread the Creed resembles our obligation to show charity. We have no power to help everyone and no *right* to help no one.

Some activists defend their position using analysis based on a two-part world of "free societies" (such as Western democracies) versus "fear societies" (such as communist or Arab totalitarianisms). Free societies have a duty to defeat fear societies, not only to advance world justice but for practical reasons: "fear societies" are war-prone, violent, and unstable. They can never be friends or supporters of "free societies." So it is morally and practically right for the free society of America to make war on a fear regime such as Saddam's.

This analysis is unconvincing because separating nations into free versus fear societies is like dividing animals into "big ones" and "small ones." Important distinctions get lost. A nation like France is free, but it is also a pacifist-appeasement society. The French government treats its own citizens justly, by and large—which doesn't prevent it from collaborating with governments (such as Saddam's used to be) that treat their citizens *unjustly* and would love to harm such free societies as America. When a free society like France assists a fear society like Saddam's, it becomes an enemy of Saddam's enemies—of the Iraqi people *and* the United States. America has both fear and free societies among its enemies.

To understand the world today, we must understand the two types of enemy we face and the three-part world we live in. Ever since the end of World War I there have been losers moved by poisonous resentment and winners moved by poisonous guilt—and there has been the United States, which managed neither to lose the Great War nor to feel guilty about winning. Of course, today's Arab radicals are *not* descended from the losers of World War I, not directly. But for much of the twentieth century many of the most influential radical Arab states were supported either by Soviet Russia or by Nazi Germany; so they were tied to the apron-strings of the resentful losers of the Great War.

Anti-Americans, whether they are associated with the guilty winners or with the resentful losers, are still fascinated by Americans' bizarre tendency to believe in God.

"The most endemic irrational hatred in France," wrote the French statesman and thinker Armand Laferrère in 2006, "is directed not towards Jews but towards America, and specifically towards everything in America that epitomizes Protestant beliefs: George W. Bush, evangelical Christians, and so on."* In the months before the Iraq war in spring 2003, a Norwegian demonstrator waved a placard reading, "Will Bush go to hell?" But we don't have to go all the way to Europe to find people who are ready to denounce Bush, and by implication the Americans who support him, in religion-mocking terms. Prominent people here at home stand ready to condemn President Bush's religion as the *especially* offensive thing about him. The president's religious faith is "the American version of the same fundamentalist impulse that we see in Saudi Arabia, in Kashmir, and in many religions around the world."

Those aren't the words of some college sophomore or fanatic Frenchman; this is former Vice President Al Gore, speaking like an unintelligent child in early September 2004. You might imagine that Gore would have been booted out of public life forever for saying what he did. At any rate, he is wrong. Radical Islam is a

*"The Huguenots, the Jews, and Me," *Azure* (Autumn 2006), p. 73.

religion of death, a religion that evidently rejoices in slaughtering nonbelievers for the sheer pleasure of it. The terrorist Abu Musab al Zarqawi, killed by coalition forces in Iraq in June 2006, once said, "We will either achieve victory over the human race or we will pass to the eternal life." And, "Anyone who stands in the way of our struggle is our enemy and target of the swords." (And by the way, "We have declared a bitter war against the principle of democracy and all those who seek to enact it.")

Unlike radical Islam, the radical Christianity known as Puritanism insisted, in the Bible's words, on *choosing life*; Americanism does too.

Puritans insisted on the famous words from the Book of Deuteronomy: "I have set before you this day life and death, blessing and curse: therefore choose life and live, you and your children!" (Deut. 30:19). In closing his famous essay of 1630, John Winthrop cites this verse from Deuteronomy, "Choose life and live!"—centering his words on the page for emphasis:

> *Therefore lett us choose life*
> *that wee, and our Seede,*
> *may live; by obeying his*
> *voice, and cleaveing to him,*
> *for hee is our life, and*
> *our prosperity.*

No Muslim fanatic could have written those words. John Winthrop was a founder of this nation, we are his heirs, and thank God we have inherited his humanitarian decency along with his radical God-fearing Americanism.

CHAPTER 8

THE NEW COVENANT

ere is my chance to investigate what it all comes down to, what my topic really means. If I were a rabbi or minister, I'd probably start this last chapter with a biblical text. I'm not, but I'd like to start with one anyway. The text is familiar, from the Book of Psalms: "Except the Lord keep the city, the watchman waketh but in vain."

There are many things a rabbi could say, or a priest or a minister. But what *I'd* like to say is that the psalmist has put his finger on one of the bitterest arguments in modern American life. Is religion political? Of course I'm not asking whether religion is connected to the machinations of the Democratic or Republican Party. I mean, do the religious lives of its citizens matter to the nation as a whole? To the spiritual health and physical safety of this great American city on a hill? Or is religion on the contrary a strictly private affair? Does it *matter* if the Lord keep the city?

If you are an American and choose not to believe in Americanism, or for that matter in Judaism or Christianity or the Bible, more power to you. Religious freedom is fundamental to

America. But don't deny the facts of American history or the
Bible's centrality in America's story. Don't let your children be
taught lies about America! Don't misrepresent the Puritans (or
Lincoln, Wilson, or Truman): you may not believe in God, but
they did, deeply, and they helped shape this free nation with its
proud creed of liberty, equality, and democracy. And why (why,
why?) can't you question the wisdom of activists who want to
spread our Creed without questioning their motives? The Left
and the Right both have sins to answer for. But today American
political discourse is choked with hate—of the president and
everyone who believes in him; of orthodox religious believers
and of Christians above all. I know, you know, we all know
where that hate is coming from.

I have discussed Americanism at length; now I return to
America itself. America is a biblical republic. Many of today's
leading intellectuals and cultural leaders think otherwise. They
claim, as I have noted, that America is a secular republic and
that secularism is in fact one of the great ideas on which this nation is built.

Many American intellectuals believe that America's founders
and framers were secularist or at least not traditionally religious. With the assistance of scholars who have written on this
topic in recent years, I have tried to show that this view is false.
But modern secularists make a further assertion: that freedom
of religion and separation of church and state *imply* secularism.

This assertion is also wrong. Religious freedom is indeed a
founding and guiding principle of this nation. But this noble idea
is often misunderstood. Freedom doesn't imply indifference. "I
won't interfere" doesn't imply "I don't care." Perhaps I have no
right to interfere; nonetheless I may strongly prefer one choice or
dislike another. Parents often say, "You may choose any college

you like, any major you like, any spouse you like." That certainly does *not* mean, "We don't *care* what college you choose, what major you choose, what wife or husband you marry." The American public is *not* unconcerned about whether you choose to be religious or an atheist; whether you choose a biblical religion or some other kind. Although it respects nonbiblical religions (especially ones with their own scriptures) far more than it does atheism, it prefers biblical religion. This is a biblical republic.

The founders believed that a religious public is essential to a free nation—and by accident or on purpose, they hit on the best possible method for achieving one. If it's important that everyone eat ice cream, let everyone choose his own flavor. It's no surprise that America, with its history of absolute religious freedom, should have a far more "religious" public today than any other nation in the West. (In fact, America today may easily be a more Christian nation than Israel is a Jewish one.)

So I return to America, the biblical republic. The words and stories of the Bible are in America's ears, on its mind, in its heart; they are the wallpaper and elevator music of American life. And sometimes, especially in hard times, the background becomes the foreground and the Bible gets woven right into the stuff of American history. Every chapter in this book supports my assertion—and supports the idea that Americans have traditionally believed that "except the Lord keep the city, the watchman waketh but in vain."

In this nation's history you rarely have to dig very deep to find the Bible, even in places where you don't expect it. America is a shining beach on the edge of an ocean of Bible. Dig anywhere on the beach and you will find the Bible welling up.

In October 1897 Columbia University dedicated its Morningside Heights campus in Upper Manhattan. Columbia's eminent former president Seth Low spoke in the rotunda of the new library that had been named for him. This building, with its imposing dome and statue of Alma Mater out front, still marks the center of the Columbia campus. In the late 1960s it was the focus of campus anti-Vietnam demonstrations.

"The founders of this university," Low said, "looked upon God as the source of all wisdom, and they placed upon the college seal as its motto for all time 'In thy light we shall see light' [Ps. 36:9]. A century and a half of years almost have rolled around since then," he continued, "and the authorities of Columbia still believe that this is the spirit in which all study should be carried on. The seal of the college is set in the pavement of the corridor just outside the entrance to this room. I can hardly imagine a better motto for a library or for a university."

A hundred-odd years later, an Ivy League university has become the last place you'd look for a celebration of the Bible. But it won't always be this way. At Low Library the campus itself says what the faculty would mostly rather forget: "Except the Lord keep the city, the watchman waketh but in vain."

You don't expect to find Bible talk at the nation's universities nowadays, any more than you'd expect to find it at the front lines in a war. Perhaps there are no atheists in foxholes, but soldiers have never been known for their pious language or fondness for quoting Scripture, either.

America *was* a nation with the Bible on its mind during the Second World War. In his January 1942 State of the Union message, weeks after Pearl Harbor and the Nazi declaration of war, FDR said, "We are inspired by a faith which goes back through all the years to the first chapter of the Book of Genesis: 'God created man in His own image.' We on our side are striving to be true to that divine heritage."

Still, no one expects to hear the Bible at the front lines. That makes it fascinating to consider the best movie ever made about World War II (though not the best known, by a long shot). It dates from 1949. It's about a small American unit in the Battle of the Bulge. It's no documentary or newsreel, but art can be truer than life.

The film shows us the front lines as America pictured them, or remembered (or chose to remember) them, only a few years later. There are no generals in this movie, no one above the rank of captain. The film is about life in the freezing mud, where each day offers a fresh chance of being blown to bits by a shell or a bomb or knocked down by a bullet. It's a life where you spend all day and night in the same small group of men, including some who are your friends for life and others you can't bear, who set your teeth on edge. Without attempting to sneak one obscenity past the censors, the script produces an extraordinarily realistic impression of frontline life—where army propaganda ("You'll find a home in the army!") is casually, savagely kicked around, where disdain for the rear echelon is a steady theme, where no one has time for big statements on any topic. There are no dramatic, patriotic assertions in this movie, only a low rumble of contempt for everything the Nazis stand for and a wistfully intense love of country, part patriotism and part sheer homesickness—and both are far too deep for men to talk about.

The movie is *Battleground*, directed by William Wellman at MGM, and it centers on a beautifully balanced performance by Van Johnson that is full of underplayed wit and plain, sturdy detail that rings true. It is the story of the famous battle for Bastogne, where the Americans were surrounded by Nazis and smothered under snow and fog; but the subtext is about a young soldier seeing combat for the first time, a new replacement fresh from the States, and the man's changing attitude toward a verse from Isaiah.

As the fighting begins, the young soldier clutches his verse like a child with a security blanket: "They that wait upon the Lord shall renew their strength; they shall mount up with wings as eagles; they shall run, and not be weary; and they shall walk, and not faint" (Isa. 40:31). He knows it by heart, and his fellow soldiers (and the audience) are expected to recognize it. As the fighting continues, the casualties mount, and the danger grows, the verse seems to mock the young soldier—and he mocks it. But in the end it sees him through. The fog lifts, and the air force can mount up once again with wings as eagles, and the infantry can at last renew its strength, run and not be weary, walk and not faint.

In the end the young soldier decides, implicitly, that it is okay to lean on the Bible, even to draw comfort where the facts don't seem to justify any. If you advance the Bible some trust and some faith, it will pay you back in the end. It will make every spiritual debt good.

And so once again we find Americans in unlikely places with the Bible on their minds, who are apt to believe that "except the Lord keep the city, the watchman waketh but in vain." These Americans believe that religious life is indeed political and that it matters to the citizen *and* the city.

Now fast-forward about fifteen years. The heroes of today's liberal Democratic Party are unlikely, you might think, to have had the Bible on *their* minds. But Martin Luther King is the largest of them all—a hero of the Left *and* of America in general. He was a minister, who talked Bible all the time.

King delivered his greatest speech from the steps of the Lincoln Memorial, at the event we remember as this nation's most important civil rights demonstration, on August 28, 1963. The most famous passage in this famous speech begins, "I have a *dream* today!" It includes these lines: "I have a dream that one day every valley shall be exalted, and every hill and mountain shall be made low, the rough places will be made plain, and the crooked places will be made straight; 'and the glory of the Lord shall be revealed and all flesh shall see it together' " (Isa. 40:4–5).

Did King believe that "except the Lord keep the city, the watchman waketh but in vain"? Did he believe that religion is political and not just private, that it matters to the nation as a whole? I think he must have.

That famous speech was delivered only a few months before another hero of liberalism was murdered in Dallas. John Kennedy spoke eloquently about the nation's duty to fight communism on behalf of Americanism. In his inaugural address in January 1961 Kennedy had said that "we shall pay any price, bear any burden, meet any hardship, support any friend, oppose any foe, to assure the survival and the success of liberty." Which is a classic statement of democratic chivalry. George W. Bush could have said exactly the same as he prepared the nation for war in Iraq. He could say it today.

Kennedy was the bridge between Eisenhower, hero of the Second World War, and Lyndon Johnson, during whose administration America started to come apart at the seams and the culture war began. Today we are a nation thick with hatred, lost in the murk.

But Kennedy and his staff wrote a speech for the president to deliver at lunch on a clear autumn day long ago, on November 22, 1963. Of course he didn't live until lunch, and this speech was in a sense his last. Its very last line was a quotation from the Psalms: "Except the Lord keep the city, the watchman waketh but in vain."

Kennedy never made the speech, never spoke the verse.

Ever since, his unspoken last words have overhung the American landscape like a heavy raincloud in a drought-stricken land. Today the biblical drought is still on, and the cloud still hangs there.

Kennedy kept a personal Bible in the bedside table on Air Force One; Johnson was sworn in using that Bible. Right after the swearing in, the Bible disappeared. An unknown stranger asked for it at the Dallas airport, and the judge who'd administered the oath turned it over. As of 1967, when William Manchester published his semiofficial book on the assassination, it had never been seen again.

Which makes a perfect, ominous picture of the end of an age: the biblical warning that is never delivered; the Bible that vanishes into the hands of somebody no one seems to know, who was wandering around the field at Dallas. One can't help thinking of verses from Job: "The Lord said unto Satan whence comest thou? Then Satan answered the Lord and said, From going to and fro in the earth, and from walking up and down in it."

Years after the assassination the Bible turned up, and today it's in the Lyndon Baines Johnson Library and Museum at the University of Texas in Austin. So this isn't really the story of a missing Bible; it's the story of a missing story. When the Bible was lost, it was a big deal; when it was found, no one cared very much anymore.

Yet that Bible is still waiting for someone to pick it up and read out that missing verse from Psalms, the silence at the center of our noisy national life: the verse Kennedy meant to read, before the culture war closed in.

Today the public is uncertain and foundering. Polls show it. On the one hand America remains strongly Christian, but knowledge of the Bible is collapsing, among young people especially. A case like Terri Schiavo's seemed to pose the simplest kind of moral question: when a person is too sick or weak to speak for herself and has made no serious plans for this contingency, is it all right to kill her? When her parents plead for her life? If it *is* all right, might it at least be okay to slip the dying woman an ice chip while she starves to death, at a time when she's suffering agonizing thirst—or *might* be? America's duly constituted legal authorities approved the killing; forbade the ice chip. And the public wasn't sure whether it agreed or not. It was a terrifying low point in this nation's moral pulse, which almost disappeared. At that moment our heart nearly stopped.

Why is the public confused? Why is it foundering? The Bible has temporarily been dismissed from American public life. We no longer have the Bible on our minds. That might be part of the reason.

Ultimately morality can get no purchase without religion; without divinity to hold on to, morality is a first-time rollerskater trying but failing to keep its rear off the floor. But today's secularists have left morality far behind and foresee a society where human rights have replaced human duties, where only the state has obligations and the passive, bovine citizenry can relax and let the government take care of everything.

But the secularists won't succeed. Granted they are succeeding in the short term: nowadays most children get little or no religious instruction. (A Bible Literacy Project survey in

2006 showed astonishing ignorance of the Bible among teenagers.) Most children get little or no instruction in plain ethics, either—and if they do, they learn *modern* ethics. Here is a passage from the last page of a recent, respected introduction to the topic: modern ethics points us toward "an increased sensitivity" to various things, "to the environment, to sexual difference, to gender, to people different from ourselves in a whole variety of ways." Modern ethics suggests that we must be "careful, and mature, and imaginative, and fair, and nice, and lucky."

Careful, mature, imaginative, fair, nice, lucky: nothing here is inspiring, noble, or even hard. Nothing here exhorts us to be generous or just; decent, honest, or kind; gracious or merciful; patriotic or brave; or loving or good.

Yet young people surely ought to know that "you must love your neighbor as yourself." "Choose life and live, you and your children!" "Man, it has been told you what is good, and what the Lord requires of you: only to do justice, love mercy and walk humbly with your God." "Justice *justice* shalt thou pursue!" "Man does not live by bread alone." "The meek shall inherit the earth." "Do not follow a multitude to do evil." These thoughts come from the Bible, from the Old Testament in fact. They come (in other words) from the book so many intellectuals despise and so many of America's founders held dear.

The next great American religious revival will start, my guess is, on college campuses—and it will start fairly soon. The need is great. In a spiritually dried-out land where "careers" alone are holy, the thirst is acute. Someone will start preaching. Audiences will be small at first, but young people want to hear this message: "Forget your career and think about your family. Forget your rights and think about your duties. Forget your bank account and think about your country. Forget yourself and think about your God." Teachers and professors, guidance counselors and deans, now tell students the exact opposite. But young people know when they are being lied to. They only need someone to tell them the truth. And someday soon some sympathetic disciple of the founding fathers will compose the indispensable companion to our Bill of Rights (which is rightly admired by the whole civilized world)—a Bill of Duties that conveys the exact same truths in terms of responsibility instead of entitlement.

Someday soon someone will remind this whole nation that tolerance is American but secularism is not. That absolute religious freedom is American but contempt for religion is not. That religious doubt is American but religious indifference is not. That heated religious debate is American but cold academic disdain is not. That chivalry is American but complacency is not. That America is a biblical republic, and Americanism is a biblical religion. And someone will take up that Bible that was lost and found, and read out the missing verse, or shout it out—and sounds of the Bible will return in full flood to the sullen cracked dry earth of American public life—and we will say with the Song of Songs, "The winter is past . . . The flowers appear in the land." We will remember that "except the Lord keep the city, the watchman waketh but in vain"; and we will once again be proud of who we are.

New Haven, 2007

INDEX

ABOUT THE AUTHOR

David Gelernter is professor of computer science at Yale University, national fellow at the American Enterprise Institute, and a former member of the National Council of the Arts. He is the author of *The Muse in the Machine, 1939: A Novel, Machine Beauty*, and other books. He has written for *Commentary*, the *Wall Street Journal*, the *Weekly Standard*, and *Time* magazine, among other publications. Gelernter lives in New Haven, Connecticut.